Students Mentoring Students

in K-8 Classrooms

Creating a learning community where children communicate, collaborate, and succeed

Diane Vetter

Pembroke Publishers Limited

This book is dedicated to my husband, who kept the home fires burning while I raced from school to university to complete my research and doctoral studies, to my children (now adults with wonderful spouses and children of their own), who reminded me when the going got tough that I was lighting a path of perseverance for them to follow, and to my grandchildren, who inspire me to reimagine education as it might be in their time.

© **2023 Pembroke Publishers**
538 Hood Road
Markham, Ontario, Canada L3R 3K9
www.pembrokepublishers.com

Funded by the Government of Canada
Financé par le gouvernement du Canada | Canadä

ONTARIO CREATES

Library and Archives Canada Cataloguing in Publication

Title: Students mentoring students : creating a learning community where children communicate, collaborate, and succeed / Diane Vetter.

Names: Vetter, Diane, author.

Description: Includes bibliographical references and index.

Identifiers: Canadiana (print) 20230223273 | Canadiana (ebook) 20230223303 | ISBN 9781551383620 (softcover) | ISBN 9781551389622 (PDF)

Subjects: LCSH: Group work in education. | LCSH: Team learning approach in education. | LCSH: Mentoring—Study and teaching (Elementary)

Classification: LCC LB1032 .V48 2023 | DDC 371.3/6—dc23

Editor: David Kilgour
Cover Design: John Zehethofer
Typesetting: Jay Tee Graphics Ltd.

Printed and bound in Canada
9 8 7 6 5 4 3 2 1

Contents

Acknowledgments *6*

Introduction *7*

Chapter 1: **It Always Begins with a Question…** *11*

> *How might we find innovative ways to engage our students in collaborative classroom talk that fosters greater thinking, learning, and community?* *12*

Links to Research *13*
Communication *14*

> *Why is it important for students to communicate with each other while learning?* *14*

Action Strategy: Talking to Learn *16*
Action Strategy: Hear What I'm Thinking *18*

Collaboration *19*

> *What is the value of classroom collaboration?* *19*

Action Strategy: Curate and Critique *20*
Action Strategy: Treasure Map to Learning *22*

Community *23*

> *How does creating community facilitate success in learning?* *23*

Action Strategy: Welcoming Voices *24*
Action Strategy: What I Bring *26*

Chapter 2: **Sharing Our Voices** *31*

Theory Meets Practice *33*
Authentic, Relevant, Meaningful, Purposeful Talk *33*

> *How might we move beyond accountable talk to make classroom conversations richer and more relevant to the individuals in our class?* *33*

Action Strategy: Talk Shows *34*
Action Strategy: Scaled Feedback *35*
Action Strategy: Learning Paths *36*

Equity and Inclusion in Collaborative Learning   40

*How might we demonstrate to students the value of actions and
reactions that are respectful, equitable, and inclusive for everyone
in our classroom community?*   40

Action Strategy: Glyphs   41
Action Strategy: Turning to Wonder   45

Mentoring Partnerships within the Community   46

*How might we facilitate flexible peer-mentoring partnerships to
build community and support student learning?*   47

Action Strategy: Podcasts   48

Chapter 3: Realities of the Classroom   51

Setting the Stage for Talk, Collaboration, and Community   53
The Physical Environment   53

*How might the intentional act of creating a community-centreed
physical space build relationships and facilitate collaborative
learning and communication?*   53

Action Strategy: Central Focus Design   54
Action Strategy: Playing Card Groups   56
Action Strategy: Lesson Baskets   58
Action Strategy: Appreciations   59

Technology and Community   61

*How might collaborative learning through technology be
effectively integrated into the pedagogy of a classroom
community?*   62

Action Strategy: What I Know   65
Action Strategy: Patterned Writing   67

Assessment outside the Box   69

*How might methods of assessment of student learning
transform to reflect the realities of a talk-rich, collaborative
community?*   70

Chapter 4: Leaders in Learning   73

Thinking about Thinking   75

*How might peer mentoring provide opportunities for students
to consistently think at a higher level and thereby increase their
capacity for learning beyond memorization?*   75

Action Strategy: Ways of Knowing   78
Action Strategy: Mathemagicians   80

An Engaged Learning Community   *81*

> *Which affective factors underpin the creation of an engaged learning community?*   *82*

> Action Strategy: Noise Meter   *84*
> Action Strategy: Bringing It Back   *86*

Living Curriculum   *88*

> *How might we bring the curriculum to life for students with varying interests and ways of learning?*   *90*

> Action Strategy: Publishing   *92*
> Action Strategy: Cross-Canada Tour   *93*

Chapter 5: Reimagining Learning for the 21st Century   *97*

> *How might we reimagine learning for the 21st century in simple ways that make a difference to student thinking and learning?*   *99*

Well-Being   *100*

> *How might we enhance students' well-being and resilience through classroom learning?*   *101*

> Action Strategy: Anchor Books   *103*
> Action Strategy: Happy Slippers Toolkit   *105*

Citizenship   *107*

> *How might we help students to embrace their roles and responsibilities as citizens both locally and globally?*   *107*

> Action Strategy: Wonder Walls   *110*

Stewardship and Legacy   *111*

> *How might we inspire students to greet the present with an eye to caring for the world they will live in as adults, and to think of the legacy that they are building?*   *111*

> Action Strategy: Nature Nurtures   *112*
> Action Strategy: Thinking Journeys   *113*
> Action Strategy: Stone Soup   *116*

Conclusion   *118*

References   *119*

Index   *121*

Acknowledgments

My sincere appreciation to Judy Blaney, Natasha Marchant, and Rhonda Robert. You consistently challenge my thinking, share your enthusiasm, and innovate in collaborative ways to enrich teaching and learning. You are amazing educators and dear friends.

To the many colleagues who have mentored me and supported my research, welcomed me into their classrooms, and shared their enthusiasm for education — thank you! Your professionalism and dedication to teaching and learning continue to make a difference in education.

Of course, to the students with whom I have shared classrooms over many years, you are always my inspiration. My deepest thanks to all of you. Indeed, you are the future!

Introduction

The seed for this book was planted over twenty years ago in an elementary school classroom in a small rural town in Ontario, Canada.

After several years of teaching English Language Learners, I was most excited, and admittedly nervous, to take on the task of teaching a grade 2 classroom. I had spent a lot of hours preparing my classroom to make it into a place that I felt would be a warm and welcoming environment for my young learners.

During the second week of school the world was shocked by a horrible tragedy. The date was September 11, 2001. Terrorists brought down the twin towers of the World Trade Center in New York City. The whole world, including my small-town school, was immersed in the news and in the horror of the event.

There was much fear as everyone wondered what the outcome of this terrible tragedy would be. No one knew what would come next, or what this devastating event would mean for peace in our world.

For our school community, it was frightening. We were situated adjacent to a large military base and many of our students came from military families. Upon hearing the news, everyone wondered what it would mean for our students, many of whom had parents who were serving in the military.

News spread quickly through the school. The grade 2 children were confused and fearful. They didn't know what would happen and they didn't know what to do. To be very honest, I felt the same way. I didn't want to further alarm a group of frightened children, but I knew we could not pretend that our classroom community was untouched by the horror.

It was clear that the planned lessons for the day were going to be totally ineffective in allaying the children's fear, and helping them through the moment. So we came together in a circle to sit on our classroom carpet and talk about how we were feeling. Most of the children articulated that they were very frightened. Many didn't know what to do, while others had bold ideas about how they would deal with "the bad guys" in superhero style.

As the children spoke, I witnessed that those who had the bold ideas were less fearful, perhaps less realistic but, nevertheless, less fearful than those who sat in tears and felt helpless. It occurred to me that we needed to do "something". I wasn't exactly sure what that "something" was, but I knew that we couldn't just sit there and be afraid.

The prior week a parent had arrived in my classroom with a donation of round stickers about 2 inches in diameter that were plain white with no printing on them. They were a donation from his company and there must have been over 2,000 stickers on a very large roll. I confess that when I first received the donation I thought, "Oh, my goodness! What will I ever do with all of these stickers?" But, I suddenly had an idea! I got down the roll of stickers and distributed at least 20 stickers to each student, along with a basket of colored markers. I rummaged through a box of old cassette tapes, and managed to find Cat Stevens' "Peace Train", which had been a favorite of mine for many years. I then explained to the children what a peace symbol was and set them the task of creating colorful peace signs on the white stickers.

As the children worked on their peace stickers, we talked about what they meant. Many of the children came from families whose parents had been on peacekeeping missions on behalf of the Canadian military so they had a good understanding of what formal peacekeeping might look like. Then we talked about the difference between being a peacekeeper and being a peacemaker. The children thought of ways that they could be both peacekeepers and peacemakers in their homes, in our community, in our school and schoolyard, and in our classroom. As they worked and talked and shared their ideas, they became calmer. They became focused on what they could do to make a difference rather than on what was happening to them as helpless beings in a frightening world.

By the time recess arrived, I can't imagine how many peace stickers our class had created. Each student set off to the schoolyard with dozens of peace stickers to share with whomever they encountered. The school custodian, the principal, the school secretary, teachers, parents who were in the school, and other students were the recipients of one or more stickers and a greeting of "peace". Everyone in the school had peace stickers on their T-shirts and even some on their arms. The principal must have received one from every student in the class as his white shirt was colorfully adorned with a multitude of stickers.

More than twenty years later, that day remains in my memory, as one of the greatest learning moments that I have had as a teacher. I learned that day that no child is too young to know that they have the power to make a difference in the world. I realized that no child is too young to be able to help another. I realized that during difficult times even the youngest child can calm or support another child, or an adult, with a kind gesture and word.

Since that day, I have made it my goal to help the students in my classrooms to support and mentor each other emotionally, socially, and academically. I have found through experience and research that peer mentoring and support is best facilitated, and most successful, when students have the opportunity to collaborate and communicate openly in the classroom. When students have the chance to engage in authentic, relevant, meaningful, and purposeful activities, when they value their own voice and the voices of others, learning for all is deeper.

The goal of this book is to tell my stories and reflect the voices of the students and colleagues who, through kind collaboration and open communication, have mentored me and each other in learning. I recognize and respect the vastness of research in education extending back centuries, and while some of the Action Strategies included here may seem to have grown spontaneously from a teachable moment, I acknowledge that reading and synthesizing education research lie at the heart of my work.

Within each chapter, you will find an approach to a theme that is supported with research, along with a retelling of my related experiences. I visualize these retellings as glimpses "through the window" into my classroom and many others that I have had the honor of visiting or participating in as a researcher. I hope the stories will be useful in bringing the theory to life in your classroom.

Finally, there will be a selection of Action Strategies that will guide you in implementing specific activities in your own classroom. Knowing that each class has a unique dynamic, the Action Strategies are not prescriptive lesson plans that are aligned with curriculum content, rather they are ways of "being and doing" in your classroom that are adaptable to fit the needs of your students and your specific learning environment. The adaptability of these Action Strategies has allowed me to implement them in elementary schools and university classrooms alike. Each Action Strategy has many possibilities to differentiate for multiple grades and levels of student learning. I encourage you to tweak them, rework them, and adapt them to suit the needs of your classroom. When we create a learning community where children communicate, collaborate, and succeed, the benefit to students, teachers, and school community is, indeed, wondrous.

1

It Always Begins with a Question…

When I began teaching, the concept of classroom communication and collaboration, particularly in the primary grades, revolved around formalized and formulaic processes or learning centres. The most common form of independent talk was Show and Tell. It remains a popular oral language strategy today, which provides our youngest learners with the opportunity to speak in a more public setting.

You likely know the routine: on an assigned day, a student is invited to bring an item from home to show to their classmates. Generally a favorite toy is selected. The student stands up in front of the class and says a few words about the toy. Prompts for the activity might include a description, where it comes from, and why it is a favorite. Then the student invites classmates to ask questions. After some awkward silence there might be one or two questions. Classmates generally revert to the tried and true questions of "Do you like it?" or "Why is it special?" Then after more silence the teacher likely concludes with, "Thank you very much", and the student goes back to their seat.

I always found Show and Tell to be a really awkward process in my classroom. Too many children were reluctant to speak at all. Others talked on and on. The talk students used was usually contrived or memorized. In my head I imagined myself walking into a room, conference, party, or wherever and saying, "Hi, my name is Diane. This is my new jacket. I got it at the mall. It came in red and it came in blue, but I bought red because I like red best. Red is my favorite color! Does anybody have any questions?" Well, I think you can imagine how totally bizarre and inauthentic that would be. Yet it was the real-life equivalent of what I was asking my students to do in my classroom. I valued the premise of using oral language in the classroom, but I knew that there had to be better ways to facilitate meaningful communication, collaborative interaction between students, and classroom community.

So I asked this question:

How might we find innovative ways to engage our students in collaborative classroom talk that fosters greater thinking, learning, and community?

I wanted my students to learn to express themselves articulately and to communicate with each other in a way that was both inviting and encouraging so that classmates would be motivated to thoughtfully respond. Importantly, I imagined the communication to be authentic, relevant, meaningful, and purposeful to those students who were engaging in the conversation. I imagined shared wondering and exploration to enrich learning. I imagined scenarios that would engage children in learning and conversation to such an extent that classroom management happened largely organically with minimal intervention from me. I didn't know where to begin.

I wanted to create a classroom environment that allowed students to mentor each other and learn from each other through rich communication and collaboration; however, my biggest fear at that time was the process of assessment. I was terrified to think how I might assess student learning. Classroom talk happens in the moment. It is easy to collect worksheets, notebooks, and spelling tests for grading. Assessing classroom talk and collaboration seemed a greater challenge. The answers that I have discovered along the way are shared in this book, along with the new wonderings that my learning has uncovered.

I have embraced my own question in much the same way that I ask students to embrace theirs in my classroom every day. I acknowledge that questions are magical because they are the keys that open doors to incredible learning, new ideas, and, importantly, more questions. If we stop asking questions, we stop learning. There will always be an infinite supply of questions if we open our minds to new learning.

As I delved into my question, I took the opportunity to keep doing what I imagine you are doing now:

- reading,
- researching,
- analyzing and evaluating,
- wondering,
- thinking outside the box,
- looking beyond what is,
- imagining, and
- creating what could be.

I also invited interested colleagues to join me in the journey of exploration. New practices and concepts are more easily implemented when you are in a co-mentoring partnership with a colleague. To fully explore my questions, I listened to, and considered carefully, conflicting opinions and ideas about classroom communication and collaboration. While taking into account alternate perspectives, I set aside the negativity of naysayers who attempted to dissuade me from pursuing the classroom that I imagined.

Having spent more than twenty years trying, succeeding, trying, sometimes failing, and trying again to find a perfect answer to my question, I have come to realize that one magic answer does not exist. I am still learning new and innovative ways to engage students. I have learned that caring and vibrant learning communities result in far greater student success. Facilitating student communication and collaboration creates the learning partnerships and mentoring relationships, both teacher-student and student-student, that benefit the classroom community and beyond.

Times change quickly and today's classroom looks very different from the one where I taught in 2001. However, some things don't change. Working with students in their development of strong communication, collaboration, and relationship-building skills that allow them to become learners who mentor each other to facilitate success for everyone in the classroom community remains a worthy objective.

In today's digital world, keyboarding has overtaken cursive writing for text-based communication. We are increasingly using voice to text in our daily lives and speaking messages into phone apps. There are more and more people listening to podcasts to seek opinions and information. People are choosing to listen to audiobooks while they walk, drive, or commute on public transit. Social media increasingly incorporate our stories through brief video recordings where messages must be clear and succinct. A few years ago, students in my classroom were writing letters to the editors of local papers in the hope of having their voices heard. Today they are creating Instagram stories and TikTok videos that appear instantaneously to a worldwide audience.

I believe there has never been a more important time in society for students to learn to communicate effectively, to learn collaboratively, and to build a learning community with each other. They need to know how to explore multiple perspectives and understand different and diverse ways of knowing and being in the world. Today, words that are carelessly spoken or thoughts that are inarticulately phrased can quickly become headline news. As educators we can't expect students to intuitively develop a high level of communicative competence or an understanding of how others think and view the world. We can and indeed we must facilitate their development through the creation of opportunities to learn to communicate effectively, learn collaboratively, broaden their thinking through shared experience in community, and analyze and evaluate what they hear and see to create new wonderings for a future that we have yet to imagine.

Links to Research

I have always found great value in looking at what others have discovered through their experience and research. In some cases what I find affirms my thinking, while in others it challenges preconceived notions. Both experiences help me to wonder more deeply and question more extensively. In this chapter, I will provide a brief overview of the theoretical background that has been foundational to my research and my work in creating, observing, and exploring learning communities where children collaborate, communicate, and succeed.

The research presented here serves as a means to ground the Action Strategies that you will find embedded in each chapter. I trust that these research insights will also support you as you analyze and evaluate the content of this book and consider it for use in your own classroom. What follows is by no means a comprehensive overview of literature, rather it is a glimpse into research that has informed my work.

As noted, the three foundational principles that this book upholds for creating successful mentoring between students in the classroom are **communication**, **collaboration**, and **community**. In my experience, observation, and research, I have found that optimal learning is created when all three factors are linked and co-exist in the learning environment. However, in terms of research perspectives, and for the sake of clarity, I have chosen to discuss each component individually.

Communication

Why is it important for students to communicate with each other while learning?

It is certainly no secret that kids love to talk. I suspect that any teacher can tell you it's true. In fact, anyone who lives near or works in a school knows that once the bell rings for recess or at the end of the school day the neighbourhood fills with laughter and young voices. The sound of schoolyard voices represents enthusiasm and fun (and, perhaps, the occasional conflict). Yet when the serious business of learning begins, voices become modulated or perhaps silenced. When I ask teachers why this is true, the majority understandably respond that this is largely about maintaining a safe learning environment. A classroom that resembles a playground may soon become chaotic. Constant noise is wearing on teachers and students alike. On the other hand, the silent classroom leaves many opportunities for thinking and learning unexplored and many students disengaged. It might seem to be an all-or-nothing conundrum, but take heart! As facilitators of learning and stewards of student well-being, teachers **can** ensure the well-being of students, meet curriculum expectations, **and** welcome lively young voices in the classroom.

Let's begin with what we know about talk …

In term of educative talk, there are two specific ways that students engage with talk. The first is **learning to talk**. This includes expanding vocabulary, using correct grammatical constructions, understanding the social implications of various types of speech, and understanding the purpose of speech in a variety of situations. When learning to talk, students come to understand the different nuances of utterances such as "Close the window!" and "Would you mind closing the window?" They learn how to use expressive language to enhance speech and, subsequently, written text. They make sense of and master the use of increasingly complex grammatical constructions. They understand that they must make meaning of talk when they are listening and create meaning with talk when they are speaking. They also learn that different discourses are used in different settings. For example, they might use one Discourse (Gee, 2008), or manner of speaking, with friends in the playground and a different Discourse with their grandparents or when presenting to a group. The combination of these facets of learning to talk allows children to develop what is referred to as communicative competence, a vital skill in daily life.

The second form of educative talk is referred to as **talking to learn**. Talking to learn can include the intentional use of techniques such as questioning or challenging an idea or concept to expand personal understanding. Other times, talking to learn can take the form of reiterating or wondering to clarify thinking processes. Talking to learn requires open-ended conversation that allows for building ideas and creating new concepts as conversations progress. While it is possible to gain new knowledge by reading a text, the interactive discussion that spurs thinking and generates new questions and subsequent learning is invaluable to moving from simple understanding to higher-level thinking.

Learning to talk means acquiring the grammatical, meaning-making, and social aspects of language. This includes learning a range of discourses (personal, professional, social, etc.) that speakers employ in different settings.

Perhaps you have to update colleagues about a new teaching strategy at the upcoming staff meeting. You make sure you can explain the policy and have explanations at hand for any new vocabulary or eduspeak that may arise. You think of questions that may be asked so you have the answers prepared.

You consider how you will present the information in an accessible and professional manner to ensure that listeners receive your intended message.

Talking to learn means using specific strategies such as questioning, wondering, and thinking aloud, to support analysis and evaluation of new information in order to engage in higher-level thinking.

If you were on the receiving end of a new teaching strategy, you might ask questions about research relating to the new strategy and why it will be valuable, or how it might impact learners. You might wonder about how the new idea relates to your current practice or what additional learning you may need to implement the strategy.

Talking to learn often results in "aha" moments and deeper understanding of new ideas, concepts, and strategies. It also generates new questions and thoughts that you may not have previously considered.

THROUGH THE WINDOW...

I recall returning to school after a day's absence. A colleague greeted me in the hall to update me on the news from the prior day. After giving me the lowdown on a couple of items, she said, "You got lucky with a supply teacher yesterday. I walked by and there wasn't a peep out of them [the students]". I tried not to look disappointed and thanked her for letting me know. You see, in my classroom, I loved the "peeps" and the low hum of little voices who were engaged in their tasks and sharing explorations with their classmates. This interaction with my colleague reminded me that not everyone shared my enthusiasm for communication and collaboration in the classroom and that much work remained to be done to ensure that learning to talk and talking to learn would flourish in 21st-century classrooms.

The gap between the theoretical value of **talking to learn** and the apparent lack of direct implementation in the classroom has drawn my attention for many years. In my research I have noted that while the foundational theories that demonstrate the value of student to student communication as a means to develop thinking continue to be highly respected, the practical implications of initiating a program that embraces student communication and collaboration continue to present challenges. Classroom talk is often restricted to scripted or prescriptive activities, such as Show and Tell. As students progress through the grades, they begin to deliver oral presentations and prepared speeches and eventually participate in formal debates. While these activities are helpful in building the communicative competence of students, in other words their ability to produce appropriate or accountable talk, they do little to support the cognitive growth that results from **talking to learn**. Despite being strongly supported (Dewey, 1916; Piaget 1923/1959; Vygotsky 1934/1986) as a proven process to develop higher-level thinking skills in young learners, talking to learn often takes a back seat in daily practice. The Action Strategy "Talking to Learn" is a good way to get students started working together.

ACTION STRATEGY: TALKING TO LEARN

What…

Talking to learn is a strategy that encourages students to use classroom talk as a tool for learning across the curriculum.

Asking students to edit a text is usually met with a deep sigh that indicates they have no desire to do so and thought they were finished writing. Yet, when asked to read their work aloud to a peer, students hear their required edits and quickly recognize that they must return to the text. It saves the teacher from being the recipient of a lot of sighs, side-eye looks, and grumbles!

In my personal experience, talking my way through something has always been my first go-to strategy. In fact, as I write this book, I read each section aloud so that I can hear how it sounds. What looked good to me on a piece of paper or screen may be misconstrued or my intention misunderstood by a listener/reader. When I read my written text aloud, it becomes clear where the written text needs edits.

Students reading their work aloud to a peer serves a dual purpose. The reader has the opportunity to hear how their own work sounds when spoken, while the listener gains insight into a different perspective. The read-aloud generally results in questioning and discussion of ways the work might be strengthened for clarity and readability.

Implementation

How…

Teachers create an environment rich in talk by facilitating opportunities for authentic talk and setting expectations for the social norms associated with classroom conversations, including creating a physical environment that welcomes small-group conversations and a focal area for whole-group discussions. Classroom communities develop protocols for what rich talk looks like, sounds like, and feels like in the classroom, establishing acceptable noise levels, along with methods for students to self-regulate during conversations.

Talking to learn is used to support investigation and exploration of new topics and/or sharing of interests and experiences connected to the learning. Such conversations heighten student engagement as they collaboratively communicate their enthusiasm for a topic.

Talking to learn is implemented to help students self-edit and critique their work and that of their peers through read-aloud of written texts. The use of a recording device can also help students as they record and replay their written work to improve rhythm, use of vivid language, and clarity of a text.

Students are made aware of developing insights into alternate perspectives as they share and question new concepts, understandings, and the experiences of others in the classroom.

Students question facts and information to become critical consumers of information who will be aware of the need to analyze, assess, and evaluate the ever-growing media input into their lives.

By opening a window into how others think about or learn a topic, students unpack new ways of thinking about the topic and develop metacognitive awareness of how they learn and how others learn so they can develop a learning plan that best suits their individual needs.

Why…

Research (Vygotsky, 1934/1986; Britton, 1970/1993; Cazden, 1988) demonstrates that talk is foundational to learning and to the development of deeper cognitive processes. Talk is the base upon which all language functions are constructed. Classroom talk also provides students with the opportunity to try on different Discourses (Gee, 2008) and develop ways to effectively articulate their meaning in a variety of situations and contexts.

What If…

What if talking to learn became the norm in the classroom and students learned to share, explore, investigate, question, discuss, agree, and disagree in respectful ways that valued alternate opinions and their potential to enhance and develop thinking in new and innovative ways?

Current oral communication theory has developed from the work of theorists who have linked oral language to thinking. Theorists provide varying insights on the means by which oral language facilitates thinking; however, they agree upon the critical links between talk and thought.

Links between oral language and cognitive development suggest that students who are in the earliest stages of reading and writing skills acquisition rely heavily on oral language to support and clarify their developing skills and learning, and to interpret their ideas, drawings, and initial attempts at writing (Piaget, 1923/1959). Conversely, limiting students' opportunities to engage in classroom communication may effectively impede their development of text-based literacy skills. Britton (1970/1993) makes explicit the connection when he states, "Reading and writing float on a sea of talk".

Moving beyond reading and writing to consider the role of talk in cognitive development, Vygotsky (1934/1986) states, "…speech is an expression of that process of becoming aware". He concludes, "Thought is not merely expressed in words; It comes into existence through them" (*Thought and Language*, 1934/1986). These foundational philosophies about the value of talk underpin my belief in the importance of classroom communication. Given that speech develops awareness, then silence in the classroom impedes that development.

ACTION STRATEGY: HEAR WHAT I'M THINKING

What...

Hear What I'm Thinking encourages students to articulate their thinking aloud to gain greater understanding, clarity, and insight into the topic or process. A teacher can use the strategy to model for students the questions that might be asked or the processes that might be undertaken to learn something new or to solve a problem. Teachers can also use the strategy to highlight the qualities of strong writing or the literary techniques of story, storytelling, or narratives.

How often have you asked a question of someone, only to find that the question is no sooner out of your mouth than the answer has popped into your head? This is a perfect example of how the oral articulation of your question facilitates the thinking process through which you then analyze and evaluate what you know to come up with the answer to your question.

"Thought is not merely expressed in words; It comes into existence through them" (Vygotsky, 1934/1986).

Implementation

How...

Hear What I'm Thinking can begin with a teacher simply stopping during a read-aloud to comment on an aspect of a text to strengthen the story for the reader. For example, in *Sister Anne's Hands*, the author describes the quiet of the classroom after a racist incident. She writes, "You could have heard a butterfly sigh for the rest of that day" (Lorbiecki, 1998). Pausing after reading this sentence aloud and asking students to visualize the moment helps them to fully internalize the reaction of the character and the power of vivid language to create emotion in a text. In a science class, a teacher might model the questions scientists or learners might ask themselves as they begin their study. During the course of a day, teachers act and react in subconscious ways. Stopping to make explicit our thinking behind the actions of and reactions to learning help students to create their own questions and develop their awareness of the thought processes that will support learning.

Why...

Vygotsky (1934/1986) describes speech as "an expression of that process of becoming aware". Providing students with the opportunity to bring their thoughts to life and to hear the teacher's thoughts come to life results in deeper and richer learning.

What If...

Often when I speak to teachers who have read my work, I worry about what I can say that they haven't already read in the book. Inevitably, what they want is a window into the thinking and experience that underpins my work. What if we told our students more stories about our experience and learning so that they might use them as jumping-off points into their own inquiries?

Collaboration

Beyond the proven value of classroom talk to enhance learning, communicative competence, and cognitive development, the importance of socialization and classroom interaction is making headlines. The impact of student isolation on learning during the global pandemic of Covid and the expansion of online learning caused many teachers to take a pause and consider the social value of students talking with and learning from each other. Recent studies are finding links between the lack of social learning experience due to the pandemic and the mental and physical well-being of children. Student engagement in learning through community building, collaboration, and communication are recognized as key factors for student success, as educators and policymakers work to address the realities of 21st-century learning.

What is the value of classroom collaboration?

Constructivist theories of education developed by Dewey (1916/1997) laid the foundation for much of the education research between 1960 and the new millennium. Dewey stated that communication constructs knowledge and common understanding, and social life is communicative; therefore, communication and social interaction are both "educative". It was a unique concept for 1916 and continues to engage teachers in conversations about the optimal learning environment over 100 years later.

Careful observation of how our students learn through social interaction, both in person and online, can help us to create 21st-century learning spaces that reflect how students engage most effectively in learning. A large percentage of our students are keen users of social media and gaming platforms. It is the 21st-century form of social interaction. Many education content developers have jumped on the bandwagon with the creation of learning games, websites, and other media that support curriculum. However, it is important to note the difference between students collaborating to expand thinking and deepen understanding and students internalizing rote learning through social interaction. True student collaboration and peer mentoring in learning meets the needs of students on both social and cognitive levels.

To maintain a high standard of learning and cognitive development, teachers need to engage with students to ensure that they are critical users of online resources and tools and text-based classroom resources. Students must be able to evaluate content and recognize issues that limit learning. When resources were confined to a school or public library, content was curated by librarians and educators. Textbooks and other classroom content were rarely challenged. In a world of social media, where anyone can create content, our students need to develop skills to assess a wide range of opinions and to analyze and evaluate what they read, see, and hear. Whether in conversation, in text, or online, students must share responsibility for being critical consumers. Of course, teachers share the greater weight of this responsibility with elementary school students; however, as students become more savvy consumers of information, they will rely less on teacher intervention.

Creating a collaborative experience that shares the responsibility for assessing and evaluating resources is demonstrated by the curate-and-critique process. Curating and critiquing provides students with the opportunity to question information and take an active role in and responsibility for their learning. It also provides the students with an authentic opportunity to analyze and evaluate information, text, and media — and to communicate their opinions with class-mates.

ACTION STRATEGY: CURATE AND CRITIQUE

What…

Students learn how to critically assess a text or source of information by considering narrative style and context, what is emphasized and what is left out, the author's background and perspective, the use of loaded words to attract attention or sensationalize, and information about where and when the text was published. In addition, they consider representation of stereo-types, tokenism, invisibility, relationships, lifestyles, and identities.

Students use 3" × 5" cards in book pockets in the back of texts or lists for online sites to detail their findings as they curate sources of information for accuracy, accessibility, inclusivity, and interest, noting comments, concerns, or issues with the resource.

Implementation

How…

The process begins with the development of an understanding by students that they are responsible for their own learning. Even the youngest students can understand the power a text has to influence their opinion. Given that a text or website may provide inaccurate, outdated, or outright false informa-tion, students must learn to question the text, the source, and the value of the text for learning. With a few simple prompts students can respond with symbols (e.g., ☺, ☺, ☹), ratings, or comments and in doing so recog-nize their power over the information or texts they read.

Prompts for the youngest students might include:
- Did this text/website help you to learn something?
- Can you make connections to this text?
- What is the writer trying to tell you?

Moving to:
- How was this text/website valuable to your learning?
- Whose voice is heard in or missing from this text?
- How is the author attempting to influence your thinking?

Why…

Anyone can create a website and "publish" text. Students can be easily misled by false information. Putting the power in the hands of the reader sets up young learners to become aware, informed, and critical readers and learners.

What If…

What if everyone took the time to consider the source of the news they read, the stories they engaged with, and the veracity of information? Fake news would largely disappear if even the youngest children learned to carefully consider who was attempting to manipulate their thinking, how, and why.

The curate-and-critique interactive learning experience extends beyond simply sharing information. It meets a key learning need for students who must sift through endless sources of facts and fake news to determine the veracity and reliability of what they read/view/hear. As students share their questions and their thinking, they become aware of how they might be influenced by a text or site. In doing so, they come to value the ability to analyze and evaluate a resource, and to value themselves as independent thinkers with the power to question online or traditional texts.

In support of independent thinkers, Bruner (1966) states, "We teach a subject not to produce little living libraries on that subject, but rather to get the student to think mathematically for himself [sic], to consider matters as an historian does, to take part in the process of knowledge getting". As students learn to immerse themselves in the learning and collaborate to assess resources and create new shared ideas and understandings, they create an environment where it becomes natural to think deeply about the source and content of their learning, rather than simply remember facts or information. Bruner's prompt to understand the importance of teaching children how to learn rather than teaching them what to learn sets teachers and peers in the role of communicative partner and mentor for learning whose ongoing sharing of experience and communication develops deeper understandings and richer learning.

Unfortunately, many students lack the confidence to actively participate in this sharing of experience. However, when provided with opportunities to speak on a familiar or highly relevant topic, student confidence grows.

THROUGH THE WINDOW...

A boy in the third grade who rarely interacted in classroom conversations was a good listener but hesitated to contribute. However, when the class was studying plants, he related to the context and suddenly came to life. His dad was an avid gardener and the two of them had spent hours preparing soil, planting seeds, and tending plants. He excitedly explained the process to his classmates and described how to use a rototiller. It was remarkable to observe the change in this child who was a reluctant writer and timid speaker.

This experience highlights the value of familiar context and allowing students to use their prior knowledge to build their confidence in ways that support their learning across the curriculum. That young student's science journal about plants may have been sparse, but his understandings were extensive. Sharing his knowledge orally with his peers enriched their learning and ensured accurate assessment by the teacher.

Building confidence through context is about scaffolding confidence and learning skills that allow students to branch out into new areas of learning and more difficult concepts. Students who experience success with initial learning will naturally broaden their interests and engage with new and unfamiliar topics of increasing complexity as confidence grows. Therefore, to provide an equitable opportunity for all students, it is important to provide context within which otherwise reticent participants can make their voices heard in the classroom.

Students who lack confidence are often reluctant to participate for fear of "not knowing". Think of how often teachers ask a question only to notice that only the students who know the answer are making eye contact. The others are staring at their desks or the floor, hoping to avoid the embarrassment of "not knowing". Now think about how student confidence might soar if "not knowing" became recognized as an opportunity for learning. Students need to know that it is okay to *not know*. In fact, "not knowing" is a great opportunity as it is the first step in learning something new. When students can visualize themselves as scientists, artists, historians, researchers, mathematicians, musicians, and more, they begin to see learning as an exploration and adventure. Not knowing then becomes a catalyst for future learning. When the question gets asked, eyes turn to wonder rather than drop to the floor. Students' sharing their questions and wonderings will generate far deeper thinking and greater learning than students' sharing their answers.

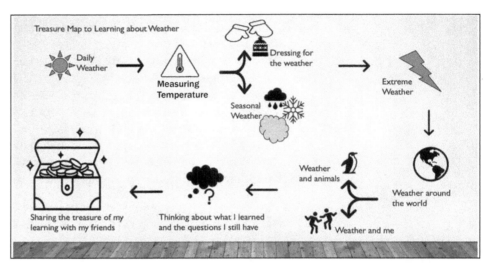

In the classroom, this map would be generated by students' questions about what they want to explore about a topic and may be hand drawn, created on a computer, or physically created on a classroom bulletin board.

ACTION STRATEGY: TREASURE MAP TO LEARNING

What…

Treasure Map to Learning turns fear of not knowing into curiosity and celebration. When beginning a new area of study, students can list what they think they know and what they think they don't know. The "know" list offers clues to what students need to investigate and confirm. The "don't know" list becomes a treasure map that leads students to engage their curiosity and explore new ideas and concepts. New learnings become unexpected treasures that students unearth.

Implementation

How…

The treasure map imagery can be brought to life on a bulletin board that helps students to guide learning throughout a unit of study. Older students may track their learning by initially imagining the route of learning, then overlaying a map of the actual path of learning that may have taken detours or unexpected side trips along the way.

Young students may enjoy making a treasure box from a recycled plastic tub or cardboard box. Each new learning is written on a piece of paper with a sparkly sticker and deposited in the box. At the end of the unit, students can open their treasure box and spread out the *gems* of learning they have collected along the way.

Why…
Curiosity coupled with enthusiasm is an unbeatable combination. The fun of a learning conquest that results in the amassing of knowledge visualized as treasure engages the imagination of learners and motivates them as they move forward in their learning. The map can act as a metacognitive guide to keep the students on track as they inquire and explore new learning in ways that suit their learning style. The culminating activity of opening the treasure box celebrates the learning and encourages students to *share their treasure*.

What If…
What if the primary objective of each new unit of study was to broaden learning skills and strengthen student curiosity using the curriculum outcomes as a treasure that opens minds and hearts to new topics and more complex learning engagements?

Socrates is quoted as saying, "The only true wisdom is in knowing you know nothing". Socrates was most insightful. If we look back even in our own lifetimes, we will see so many changes in what we knew or thought we knew about science, history, nature, space, learning, language…the list is endless. In elementary school, I carefully memorized the names of nine planets, but scientific discoveries have since determined that Pluto is merely a dwarf planet and thousands of exoplanets have been discovered beyond our solar system. Knowledge is ever changing! Therefore, Socrates' recognition of *knowing nothing* is a celebration of the limitless potential of what you have yet to learn compared to the knowledge you currently possess.

Community

How does creating community facilitate success in learning?

Expanding our knowledge and, just as importantly, our thinking does not happen in isolation. Socratic teaching relied on the interaction of students with each other and with their teacher for success. The concept of students and a teacher who invite questioning as a means of learning continues to underpin current thinking on the importance of classroom community. The word mentor is said to have originated from the root *men-*, which means to think. It is also linked to Greek mythology that names Mentor as a guide. Therefore, it is apt that students who communicate and collaborate to guide and support each other in learning and deeper thinking should be named mentors.

When students mentor each other within a classroom community, the role of the teacher necessarily changes from director of learning to facilitator, guide, and mentor. This requires willingness on the part of the teacher to engender an environment where students feel there is equity of opinion in classroom conversations. Within such an environment, students feel free to participate without censure or ridicule from others. Students also feel safe in making mistakes and taking risks with learning.

Cazden (1988) warned that regardless of good intentions, traditional patterns of student/teacher interaction may impact a student's willingness to speak and/or take risks with learning within the classroom community. For example, classroom conversations often begin by the teacher asking a question, then nominating a speaker who has raised a hand to indicate their wish to respond. Following the student's response to the question, the teacher provides an evaluative comment, such as, "Good! Thank you!" Or "Yes, that's right". The teacher then proceeds to nominate a second speaker and the pattern repeats. While well-intentioned as a strategy to include students in classroom conversation, the powerful means by which the teacher is able to control and assess each exchange in a conversation is not conducive to creating a collaborative and supportive classroom in which students become empowered to communicate their own meaning and collaborate in sharing their personal perspectives. In many cases, students will simply try to respond with the answer that they feel the teacher is seeking. This unintentional power over the community talk may give some students the impression that their voices are not welcome.

ACTION STRATEGY: WELCOMING VOICES

What…

Welcoming Voices reminds us of the responsibility to ensure that all voices are welcomed, heard, and valued in the classroom. It must be made explicitly clear by the teacher in both words and actions. Certainly some students will be more reluctant to speak and others will need a reminder to share the floor. However, it is the role of the teacher to facilitate equity in classroom conversations rather than wield control over the talk.

Implementation

How…

The teacher's conscious awareness of student voice in the classroom ensures that students feel comfortable in making their voices heard. Asking open-ended questions is a good way to begin. If a student is expected to provide a "yes/no" response or the "right answer", then they are receiving the message that they should deliver what the teacher expects to hear. Comments such as, "I am interested in knowing what you think about…" or "It is always great to hear new ideas and ways of thinking about…" communicates to students that the teacher is truly interested in what they have to say. Following a student's comments, try to avoid an evaluative remark, even a positive one. It is better to thank a student for sharing their thoughts and asking if anyone else would like to do so, thereby lessening a student's fear of being judged in front of their classmates. For whole class discussions, work with students to determine an agreed-upon system and a common understanding of social cues to ensure that students are not talking simultaneously. Visualize a civil and respectful forum rather than a question period.

Why...

The opportunity to share voices in a public forum is becoming increasingly available through social media. Learning to articulate their thoughts clearly and carefully and in a controlled manner will be of lifelong benefit to students in both academic and social settings.

What If...

What if the ability to listen effectively, speak clearly, form a thoughtful question, and formulate a respectful response were modelled and explicitly integrated into every learning interaction?

THROUGH THE WINDOW...

During a research project in a primary classroom, children were encouraged to use our time together to share their ideas and thoughts freely, rather like sharing a meal and talking about things that interested us. One little girl indicated that she never spoke during a meal. Her parents talked about what had happened at work, but she never said anything and her brother just kicked her under the table.

Then I thought about my own kids, who were teens at the time. When they were quiet at the table was it because the adults monopolized the conversation about our day? Making space for all voices and ensuring children know their voices are welcome is important for learning and for strong relationships both at home and at school.

In classroom situations, it is not always the teacher who is the controlling voice. Often there are students who are more confident than their peers or are simply more gregarious and are eager to speak out. This then leads to some students feeling excluded or intimidated.

THROUGH THE WINDOW...

Researching in a primary classroom, I audio-recorded groups of students in conversation, then gave them the opportunity to listen to their conversation and think about what they said or how they spoke. One very outgoing grade 1 student was somewhat subdued after listening to her group's recording. When I asked her what she was thinking, she told me that after listening to the recording she realized that she was "greedy" with the talking time. When I asked her to explain a bit more, she said that she had heard her voice a lot more often on the recording and some of her friends didn't get much time to speak. In subsequent group conversations, I noticed that she was still an active participant but was conscious of sharing the talk time in her group. It is important to note that the student self-regulated her behavior after hearing the recording. She understood the problem and she made a conscious effort to ensure that others had their share of talking time during group conversations. Students blossom when a classroom community is willing to listen to, and recognize the value of, all voices.

This experience of the first-grade learner, along with my earlier recount of students self-editing their work after reading it aloud, are examples of *minimal intervention* on the part of the teacher to mitigate classroom behaviors. When students are able to determine for themselves the ways of being and doing in the classroom that support their learning and that of their peers, they begin to take responsibility for the climate and the work of the community. The teacher's role in controlling or managing the classroom lessens as students develop conscious recognition of how their actions impact the environment.

Learning is full of successes and challenges. Students need to feel comfortable in experiencing both in the classroom. Most students will be able to clearly identify their struggles, but many will be less accustomed to celebrating the strengths that they bring to the community. Identifying their strengths not only builds students' confidence but also makes clear to them the tools that they already have at their disposal when they face learning challenges. Struggling with a math problem might raise feelings of "not being good at math", but thinking of persistence or patience as one of their strengths can help turn that feeling into "I can do this". The Action Strategy "What I Bring" makes explicit the importance of the strengths that each person contributes to building an inclusive learning environment. By celebrating the qualities, characteristics, and talents that each of them brings, students feel empowered to take leaps of faith in their learning and classroom interactions. The strategy also reminds students that others have different gifts that they bring to the classroom and reciprocal sharing of strengths helps everyone to learn more readily.

Peer-mentoring relationships within the classroom are not fixed. They are flexible and changing. It is important that all students see themselves as mentors to and mentees of a number of peers. Often students presume that only those with strong curriculum subject-specific skills can effectively mentor another. That is not so. Strong listening skills and patience are just as valuable in a mentoring relationship. For example, in the Action Strategies "Talking to Learn" (see p. 16) and "What I Bring" (see below), having an interested and engaged listener who remains focused as a student reads their work aloud allows the reader to self-assess their work and find areas that need improvement. Similarly, in a problem-solving situation, the role of the mentor is not to have the answer; rather it is to work as a partner to raise questions, wonder aloud, and offer an alternate lens on the problem. Students who are able to recognize their strengths are more confident in working alongside their peers as mentors and mentees in learning.

ACTION STRATEGY: WHAT I BRING

What…

What I Bring is a celebration of students' talents, skills, personal characteristics, and abilities. Using a large blackline drawing of a tree on chart paper, students add colorful sticky notes with words that demonstrate what they bring to the classroom. The finished product demonstrates the multitude of skills, talents, and personal characteristics that the class has to share with each other. Through a visual image of a tree full of brightly colored fall leaves that highlights each person's contribution, the classroom community sees that they are richer for the diversity and the abundance of the gifts they have to share with each other. The result is an affirming activity, that builds confidence, community, and collaboration.

The use of brightly colored sticky notes to represent fall leaves highlights the unique value of each quality or characteristic that students bring to the classroom.

Implementation

How…

Begin by drawing or printing the outline of a tree with multiple branches on a piece of chart paper. Distribute colored sticky notes (half size are best) that will represent the leaves on the trees. Alternatively, you can cut leaf shapes using various fall colors. Students take as many leaves as they want, filling each with one or two words to describe a talent, skill, or personal characteristic that they bring to the classroom community (patience, kindness, art, computer programming, dance, singing, helpfulness, excitement, enthusiasm, curiosity, friendship, etc.). It doesn't matter if there is repetition. There can never be too much kindness or curiosity. Once the tree is complete, the teacher can read off all the gifts the community brings. The teacher might comment, "Wow! So many of you bring kindness as a gift. We can never have too much kindness. And we have singers, dancers, poets, writers, and so many more gifts in our community. This will be a wonderful year."

Helping students to recognize shared values and understand that there is not one gift that outshines the others strengthens the community.

Why...
The start of a new year can be anxiety-producing for students who may feel insecure in moving to a new grade and a different group of classmates. What I Bring allows every student to realize that they can contribute to the classroom community and that their gift matters. The activity enhances everyone's sense of belonging and allows students to get to know each other as they talk about their gifts and share what they bring.

What If...
What if we let this idea of people having multiple and shared gifts spill over into learning? Nobody owns an idea. Often people come up with similar ideas. The classroom is enriched by sharing everyone's gift. A gift does not have to come in a box. A gift can be an idea or story that is shared, a kind word, or a helping hand of friendship.

In response to students' increasing awareness of their strengths and needs, along with those of their classmates, teachers may wish to consider providing students with more independence in the classroom. For example, within a classroom community a teacher may designate spaces where students can choose to go when they need to work independently. In addition, classroom routines can be discussed and enacted collaboratively to facilitate independent actions by students. For example:

- ✓ Students may signal the teacher and put their *name flag* in a pocket by the classroom door if they need to slip out to use the bathroom, get a drink of water, or just stand quietly in the hall to breathe.
- ✓ In online environments, students may feel free to pause their cameras if they feel overwhelmed or need a break.
- ✓ Students may be encouraged to share concerns that might impact their learning, whether it be the arrival of a new sibling, the loss of a pet, or other concerns. When the classroom functions as a community, empathy is an important component of the dynamic.

Initially, students leaving the classroom may require explicit conversation about student responsibility. There are those who will step out more frequently. Some simply need more frequent breaks, others may take advantage of a new freedom. Like all new routines, it may take a few days for everyone to adjust; however, once that adjustment is made students embrace the responsibility and the perceived autonomy to control their learning environment.

Occasionally, there are students in the classroom who need more than just a moment, or struggle with knowing when it is time to step away from the learning. At those times, teachers need a fallback plan.

There is no such thing as a perfect model of collaborative experience in the classroom. Like all communities, classrooms will have their share of conflicts that need to be resolved. Taking time to step away from conflict and come back to problem-solving through open and respectful communication with a calmer and cooler head is a useful strategy that ensures resolution while avoiding heated discussion. Not every issue has to be resolved in the moment. Students will come to understand the value of stepping away from frustration and conflict, reflecting on what happened, and then attempting resolution. When issues arise, taking time to de-escalate situations and emotions before addressing issues helps to bring about resolution and allows for talking things through with calmer heads and clearer perspectives.

When discussing conflict resolution strategies, a helpful analogy that reso-nates with students is sharing the story about a trained falcon that is released by its trainer to fly around as a mascot at sporting events. When the trainer blows a whistle, the falcon returns to the trainer's wrist to be hooded and returned to its cage. Similarly, the story of Pavlov's dog that salivated when a bell rang demon-strates how easy it is for us to rise to the bait when someone says or does some-thing that we find upsetting or contradictory to our beliefs. Whenever students complain that another student "made me angry" or justify inappropriate behav-ior with "they made me do it", teachers can simply ask, "Did they ring a bell or blow a whistle?" This generally breaks the ice to help a student realize that while they cannot necessarily control another person's actions, they have the power to control their personal reactions.

When everyone is ready and conflict resolution begins, students who have considered the other person's perspective and their own role in the conflict or concern can be reminded to use "I" statements that explain their own feelings, rather than accusatory "you" statements that hurt the other person's feelings.

Creating a classroom community has always been my priority in teaching regardless of the grade or level. From the first day of class, I dedicate time and energy to provide opportunities for relationship-building and community. I often hear the comment that the curriculum is so extensive that teachers don't have space in a day for creating community. I would respond that a classroom that disregards the creation of community experiences far greater time lost through-out the year due to interpersonal issues, disruptive behaviors, and disengage-ment with learning. The following anecdote supports my thinking.

THROUGH THE WINDOW...

The teacher was attending a professional development workshop and a supply teacher was booked for the elementary school classroom. The school secretary recounted that at 9:15 she buzzed the classroom on the intercom to ask for the attendance to be sent to the office. The students responded that the teacher wasn't there, so she asked where the supply teacher was. The students responded they didn't have one. The principal immediately went racing up the hall to the classroom door. Inside he found all of the students engaged with learning. The weather and calendar had been updated on the board. Students were working with math manipulatives or involved with one of the ongoing projects in the room. The pizza money had been col-lected and was sitting on the teacher's desk.

Who knows how long (or if) that calm might have lasted had the prin-cipal not arrived, but the situation did demonstrate that these students saw themselves as responsible members of their learning community. With-out adult intervention, they saw the work of the classroom as meaningful, important, and engaging. So, they simply got down to it.

Building community in the classroom is the best investment that a teacher can make to ensure student success. Research proves that communication, col-laboration, and community, the three focal strategies of this book, are of great value independently and collectively in supporting student learning. When implemented together, they become the superfood that feeds greater learning and deeper thinking and prepares students to thrive in a world where knowing how to learn eclipses knowledge that changes and grows exponentially each day.

2

Sharing Our Voices

If you have read the introduction to this book, you may be wondering what happened for the rest of the year with that class of grade 2 students who supported each other and the school community after the tragic fall of the World Trade Center in 2001. Those "children" are now adults, some with children of their own. Here is the story of our year together.

My father was a man with much wisdom and sound advice that he shared with me in his lifetime. He always advised me to "Start the way you mean to finish!" In the case of my young students in the fall of 2001, we continued and finished the year in the way that we had begun, by taking on challenges, talking through our problems and concerns, collaborating with each other, creating community, and making our voices heard.

Those children and their willingness to embrace classroom talk, collaboration, and community inspired me to undertake two extensive research studies that are foundational to the work that I do today.

When I look back now on that year together, it seems amazing to me just how young those children were. Some were only six years old, others had turned seven earlier in that calendar year. Yet they were so dedicated to the learning, eager to collaborate, and always ready to talk. Perhaps it was our early experience of being in the classroom together to hear the news of the terror at the World Trade Center; perhaps it was the community relationship that quickly formed as we created those hundreds of peace stickers and distributed them within our school community. I will never really know. What I do know is that we became a community of learners with much enthusiasm and respect for each other. We were a team and we felt there were no limits to what we could accomplish together.

Having begun the year talking about the importance of peace in our world, the class naturally responded to conversations about fairness and equity. We talked about the importance of inclusion in our classroom and the value of supporting each other. It was later in my research that I began to see that the students in that classroom were not merely friends or classmates. They were mentors to each other, as I was to them and, in many ways, they were to me. I would not be writing this book if those children had not left me in awe and wondering how I might replicate in years to come that experience of community, collaboration, and rich talk in the classroom. They were the catalyst that led me to want to know so much more about teaching and learning.

It was this experience of community in that fateful year that convinced me to undertake most seriously the work of relationship-building right from the first day of class every year ever since. Every time I set foot in a new classroom my first objective is to create opportunities for the students to begin the relationship-building process. I never consider time spent in creating a classroom community to be time taken away from learning. On the contrary, I see that time spent as most valuable in preparing a learning platform that will serve all the students throughout the upcoming year.

So what did we do for the rest of the year?

We opened our classroom doors to parents and others who visited us to talk about their lives. We learned about peacekeeping from the father of a student who had recently returned from the Middle East on a peacekeeping mission. We learned about the importance of pets to our well-being during a visit from a family member who trained dogs and explained to us how dogs can help people with physical and mental health concerns. We read a wide variety of interesting stories with social justice themes and talked about everything that interested us.

In talking to learn, we also learned to talk. The children developed understandings of the power of words to hurt and to heal, to make meaning and create understanding. To prepare for our classroom guests we discussed the social implications of talk, how to make others feel welcome in our community, and how to ask open-ended questions that invited others to respond.

THROUGH THE WINDOW...

At the end of every school year, our school always held a Volunteer Appreciation Tea for the people who had given their time to help our school. The principal set up tea and cookies in the library to show the school's appreciation. My grade 1 class was invited to sing a song for the volunteers.

I thought long and hard about what we would sing. It needed to be simple enough for the students to master, but I wanted it to be representative of the work we had done together as a class that year. I chose "One Small Voice Can Teach the World a Song" (Moss, 1989). We played the Sesame Street version so the children could sing along with it. We practiced and practiced. By the day of the Volunteer Appreciation Tea, we were ready.

The children walked into the library and all the volunteers were waiting. The students sang beautifully and stood politely enjoying the applause after their song. Once people had stopped clapping, the principal asked students what they had learned that year. A few hands went up. One child mentioned learning to read, another to write, another to do "pluses". Then, one child raised his hand and said to the principal, "I learned that I could make the world a better place" (Vetter, 2008). It was a remarkable moment.

As teachers, we all have those moments when we just feel that "Yes, this is where I was meant to be in this world, and this is what I was meant to do." That was the moment for me. I have never forgotten that day or what that one small voice taught me and the others in the room. To all the children who have taught me so much over the years, thank you for the learning and the questions and the understanding that we can all make the world a better place.

Theory Meets Practice

I have been to so many teacher workshops over the years and have watched countless videos on classroom teaching techniques trying to find things that worked for me. Often, I noticed that research may have been done with a small group of students. Sometimes I wondered if anyone had successfully applied these various strategies in a portable classroom at the far end of the schoolyard with limited space for students and resources, in a classroom with students who have a diversity of life, social, and cultural experiences, and special needs — in other words, in a classroom like mine. So I began to consider how I might adapt existing, proven theories to the needs of my students.

Authentic, Relevant, Meaningful, Purposeful Talk

Curriculum theory about classroom talk generally focuses on accountability. Accountable talk refers to talk that is meaningful, respectful, and mutually beneficial to both speaker and listener. It also refers to accountability to the community of learners in terms of talk protocols, the knowledge shared, and accepted standards of reasoning (Michaels et al, 2008). While I fully support the use of accountable talk that is meaningful, respectful, and mutually beneficial, I wanted the talk my students engaged in to offer more.

I wanted:

- talk that was purposeful beyond internalizing curriculum understandings;
- talk that allowed my students to take ownership of their learning and resulted in higher-level thinking;
- talk that was authentic to the interests and social understandings of my students;
- talk that celebrated and honoured the thinking, questioning, and wondering of all learners in my classroom.

So I asked this question:

How might we move beyond accountable talk to make classroom conversations richer and more relevant to the individuals in our class?

In my research, I chose the term "rich talk" (Vetter, 2009) to describe classroom talk that extended beyond accountable talk. Rich talk is **authentic** and **relevant** to the interests of speakers and listeners. Rich talk is **meaningful** to student experience and understanding, and it is undertaken within a **purposeful** activity or task that reaches beyond meeting a curriculum expectation.

Role-play activities are a good example of one way to open the door to rich talk while supporting curriculum-based learning. Role-play activities provide authentic and relevant platforms for students to represent their opinions, learning, and experience. They also open a window into the understanding of alternate perspectives. In addition, role play demands critical thinking as students assess and evaluate the knowledge, information, and perspectives from which opinions that support their role are derived. Curriculum-based objectives for literacy, numeracy, social studies, arts, well-being, and science are easily linked to topics and issues that are relevant to the students, which in turn supports engagement in conversation and motivation for inquiry. The curriculum underpins the lesson, while the rich talk, collaboration, and community engagement support the development of higher-level thinking and communicative competence.

This is how it works:

ACTION STRATEGY: TALK SHOWS

What…

Using role play or dramatizations is always a fun way to engage in rich talk that is authentic, relevant, meaningful, and purposeful to the students. One of the most popular ways to do this is to produce a "Talk Show". Within a group, one student acts as the talk show host and the others are guests invited to provide a range of opinions on an issue.

Favorite topics for students might be cell-phone use in the classroom, or owning a pet. Playing the role of teacher, parent, student, psychologist, or other expert to discuss the various opinions on the issue, students are responsible for researching and presenting an accurate perspective for their character. The final presentation provides many engaging and insightful moments for participants and their peers who participate as the studio audience.

Implementation

How…

The format can be either a roundtable or sofa-style format created using classroom chairs. Students are divided into groups and choose a topic for discussion. Teachers support students by providing suggestions for topics of interest that link to curriculum (use of technology, climate issues, etc.). Students prepare their opinions through research. The presentation is scheduled with the class as audience. The teacher may choose to record the "talk show" to allow the students to self-assess their research, information, and performance using the Action Strategy: Scaled Feedback on p. 35.

Why…

Many students will enjoy the opportunity to step outside themselves and role-play a character. To prepare for the role, students engage in inquiry, consider and develop perspective, and prepare articulate presentations using appropriate language related to the setting and topic. A student role-playing a teacher, parent, or school administrator has the opportunity to see a different perspective on an issue or concern.

What If…

Role play might be extended to characters in a book, historical personages, or community leaders, or used in preparation for an authentic and respectful discussion with school administration about a school event, social media policy, etc. Follow-up activities might include writing letters to local government regarding a community issue, or to a corporation regarding a product concern and indicating student awareness of multiple perspectives.

In reference to classroom talk, the terms **meaningful** and **purposeful** relate to curriculum, but also reflect how students define work that allows them to feel they are making a difference in their classroom, their community, or the world as they put their learning to use. Building strong professional relationships in the first days of school supports teachers in understanding the contexts that will be meaningful and purposeful within the specific classroom environment.

Activities that are **authentic** and **relevant** are key to student engagement, regardless of whether the activity is talk- or text-based. Students learning history need to see important links to current events. Students learning to write stories, poems, letters, or procedural texts need an authentic audience to find intrinsic motivation to create, edit, rewrite, and continue to improve their output. Facilitating peer mentoring and feedback in the classroom allows students to discuss their work, find new inspirations and ideas from their classmates, and collaborate with each other to encourage greater success.

ACTION STRATEGY: SCALED FEEDBACK

What…

Providing peer feedback is difficult for both children and adults. An interesting way to avoid this conundrum is through the use of a scaling question that asks the student to rate their own work prior to receiving any feedback from a peer or teacher.

An emoji scale of ☹ 😐 🙂 works for a young learner, while a rating scale of 1 – 5 or 1 – 10 works best for older students.

Having rated their own work, the peer or teacher asks for the student author/creator's insights into how they might improve their work to move up to the next level on the rating scale. The goal is to make small concrete improvements to move the rating from 3 to 4 or 😐 to 🙂, generating a discussion in which both partners can participate.

Implementation

How…

Students work in pairs to share their work with a partner. The partner views/reads the work to ensure familiarity, but does not provide immediate feedback. The student who created the work rates it using a visual or rating scale, then shares the rating with the partner and provides a rationale for the rating. The partner acts as a sounding board, but does not rate or critique the work. The partner then asks the student to provide concrete ways to improve their work by just one point on the rating scale. Both partners can then engage in conversation to discuss the student's ideas for improvement and collaboratively brainstorm.

Why…

When students receive feedback from a teacher, they often fail to take ownership and apply the feedback to future tasks. When they are asked to review, rate, and provide feedback for improvement on their own work, they relate to that experience the next time. The process also demonstrates to students that they are capable of improving their work without teacher intervention, and that they can take responsibility for doing so.

The simplest way to implement a lesson that provides students with authentic, relevant, meaningful, and purposeful learning in the classroom is to use a Learning Path.

Students begin their journey on the learning path by making connections to the topic. Making a connection sets a comfort level for the next steps. Regardless of the topic, students are never blank slates. They may not yet have extensive knowledge, but they will have connections or ways in which their personal experience has touched or been touched by the topic.

ACTION STRATEGY: LEARNING PATHS

What…

Connections / Knowings / Wonderings / Explorations / Sharing / Creating New Wonderings

A Learning Path is a route to learning that identifies phases or steps to learning along the way. Beginning with connections that welcome students into the learning and ending with new wonderings that highlight the importance of ongoing learning and deep thinking, Learning Paths demonstrate how students are leading their journey and mentoring their peers.

Implementation

How…

Learning Paths begin with a connection that builds student confidence to engage with the learning. Once connections have been made, the children may naturally move to **knowings,** or prior knowledge, about the topics. This step along the path provides the opportunity to move to an activity such as creating a poster or map of what students *think they know* on chart paper or brown paper taped to a desk or work table. It is important for students to feel comfortable adding information that they believe is accurate, even if it may be challenged in the **wonderings** stage, where students will have opportunity to examine their knowings to discover the inaccuracies of any prior understandings. **Wonderings** is where much of the higher-level thinking begins. Students look at what they know and question how they know it. They might seek out other learners to see how their understandings may be similar or different. If they have differing conclusions, students can plan out steps to analyze and evaluate what they thought they knew using the steps in the Curate and Critique Action Strategy from Chapter 1 (see p. 20). This is also an opportunity for students to discuss the process of learning. What ways might they use to undertake the upcoming **explorations** phase? How might they find alternate perspectives or ways of knowing? Whose voice has influenced their understanding and whose voice is missing from their understanding? As students engage with the process of wondering, they find themselves acting as critical thinkers. They learn to generate questions that will further lead them in developing their understandings. Following the exploration phase, students consolidate their understandings through **sharing** with and mentoring peers to create **new wonderings** that will inspire future learning.

Why...
Learning Paths engage students in authentic, relevant, meaningful, and purposeful conversation that facilitates the development of cognitive processes, supports metacognitive awareness, and provides for collaborative uses of language to make and share learnings and meanings. It makes explicit to students a system of inquiry that can be applied in the future.

What If...
The sky is the limit in adapting this strategy to new ways of thinking, wondering, exploring, and sharing learning.

Using connections to lead to new learning works for learners of every age. For example, new developments in nuclear fusion have recently been in the news. Yet if you told me we were going to discuss nuclear fusion I would probably clam right up. It is not a familiar topic for me. However, if you asked me to make connections, I could tell you about the recent articles I read, that I vividly recall the Chernobyl disaster in the news, and that I was on a canoe trip along a powerful and picturesque river and was astounded to see a nuclear power plant on the pristine shore.

A primary student might ease into the topic of plants, for example, with these connections:

✓ My family goes to the community garden to plant vegetables.
✓ I saw a show about plants on TV.
✓ I help my mom water our houseplants.
✓ We eat lots of vegetables at our house.
✓ I like fruit but not vegetables.
✓ We live near a forest with lots of trees and plants.
✓ I see weeds, grass, and big trees from my balcony.
✓ We have a rabbit in our neighbourhood that eats everyone's flowers.
✓ I saw a dandelion grow through a crack in the sidewalk.

As the connection conversation progresses, enthusiasm for the learning grows and students are able to transition to the next stage in their learning path.

Once connections have been made, students may naturally move to **knowings** about the topics. This is also referred to as prior knowledge. This step along the path provides the opportunity to move to an activity such as creating a poster or map of what students *think they know* on chart paper or on brown paper taped to a group of desks or a table. It is important for students to feel comfortable adding information that they believe is accurate, even if it may be challenged in the **wonderings** stage.

Knowledge is a product. **Knowings**, a noun constructed from an action, suggests more fluidity and openness to change. Did you know that *knowings* is a valid word in Scrabble worth 16 points?

Wonderings is where students look at what they know and question how they know it. This is where students have opportunity to examine their knowings to discover the inaccuracies of any prior understandings. They might seek out other learners to see how their understandings are similar or different. As they encounter differing data and/or conclusions, students can plan out steps to analyze and evaluate what they thought they knew. Students gaining new understandings from this process can employ the curate-and-critique strategies (see p. 20) to help them consider the veracity of new information. This is also an opportunity for students to discuss questions about the process of learning, such as:

- How might they find alternate perspectives or ways of knowing?
- Whose voice has influenced their understanding and whose voice is missing from their understanding?
- How might they confirm this information?

As students engage with the process of wondering, they find themselves acting as critical thinkers. They learn to generate questions that will lead them further in developing their understandings.

During the **wondering** phase students should be encouraged to think about the language they use in questioning themselves and each other. Many teachers use the "Q Chart", which demonstrates how to create questions that elicit progressively higher-level thinking. Level 1 questions result in information or retrieved data, Level 2 questions result in basic analysis, Level 3 questions result in analysis and prediction, and Level 4 questions reflect thinking skills that require students to evaluate information and create new thinking. While many teachers use these questioning skills when preparing their own questions, it is important for students to understand how to create higher-level questions when they are researching a topic or assessing their work.

Q-Chart						
	Is	**Did**	**Can**	**Would**	**Will**	**Might**
Who						
What						
When						
Where						
Why						
How						

	Level 1
	Level 2
	Level 3
	Level 4

The Learning Path supports opportunities for communication, collaboration, and community in the classroom. Connections, knowings, and wonderings support students as they make their thinking visible to their partner or group. Particularly in the younger grades or for students who struggle to put their thinking down on paper, these steps help students to clarify their thinking and scaffold their understandings as they lay the foundations for new learning.

The next phase on the Learning Path is **explorations**. This is where the students set out to address their wonderings, confirm or reject their prior understandings, investigate their assumptions, and explore new information and thinking. Having begun the learning process collaboratively by communicating with their peers through the first steps, students may be ready to move independently into the explorations section of the Learning Path. This is not a one-size-fits-all process. Some students may require ongoing mentoring from a partner or teacher to keep them on track and enthused as they begin to take ownership of their learning and ability to self-motivate. Others may prefer the opportunity to delve into a website, use manipulatives, or do research alone before coming back for the **sharing**. During the explorations phase students should be reminded to continue questioning and wondering.

Sharing is an important step for the communicative and collaborative aspects of the learning. Whether students are solving a math problem, undertaking a research project, or writing a story, sharing allows students to learn from each other and to develop an understanding that there are many ways to look at a topic or an issue. While it may seem evident that 3+3=6, there are many pathways to solving the problem. Allowing students to witness other ways of knowing and doing will support them in determining how they learn best and which strategies help them to be most effective in their learning, and this is the foundation of metacognitive awareness.

The final step, **new wonderings,** provides the opportunity for students to fully use their developing abilities to discuss, share, and challenge what they are learning. In a classroom community where students are collaborating and communicating with rich talk, challenges to their own thinking and that of others does not become a conflict or a deficit. Rather it is a launch point for further collaboration and communication within the community.

Learning Paths engage students in authentic, relevant, meaningful, and purposeful conversation that facilitates the development of cognitive processes, supports metacognitive awareness, and provides for collaborative uses of language to make and share learnings and meanings. Through rich talk students have the opportunity to consolidate their thinking and articulate their understandings in a supportive and inclusive environment. The opportunity for diverse and multiple wonderings allows each learner to spotlight their connections and their strengths while celebrating those of their peers. In addition, the collaborative nature of the learning and the satisfaction of learning both jointly and independently strengthens the community as students begin to see themselves as a team of learners who mentor each other.

Learning Paths focus on the student as a meaning maker and communicator with the teacher acting as a collaborative partner and as a model of and catalyst for learning. Implemented within a supportive classroom environment that values the voice of all students, Learning Paths engage students and teachers in learning through the facilitation of collaborative communication.

Equity and Inclusion in Collaborative Learning

> If the student is understood as occupying a dwelling of self, education needs to enable the student to look through window frames in order to see the realities of others and into mirrors in order to see her/his [*sic*] own reality reflected.
>
> — Emily Style, 1988

This quote by Emily Style creates an idea of the student "occupying a dwelling of self", a home. The next step is to visualize all the student "homes" coming together to build a classroom community, a place where we all belong.

Students and teachers should be able to look into a virtual mirror to see reflected their faces, stories, ways of knowing and being in the world, along with their interests, wonderings, and understandings. Through the virtual windows of the classroom, every person in the classroom should all be able to recognize and honour the diversity of the community.

So I asked this question:

How might we demonstrate to students the value of actions and reactions that are respectful, equitable, and inclusive for everyone in our classroom community?

To begin to nurture and shape an invitational, respectful, equitable, and inclusive classroom environment, the teacher becomes the first model for classroom interactions. Teachers who speak to students in a respectful manner will find that tone reciprocated. Teachers who allow student voices to be heard will, in turn, witness students who listen. Teachers are models for more than content or curriculum learning. They are also models of communication, courtesy, and respect. By being so, they can support an equitable and inclusive learning environment.

The first order of business each year is always learning our students' names. As a classroom community it is important to know if William prefers Bill, or if James prefers Jamie. One of the challenges for students of all ages, and for some teachers, is names that are unfamiliar and difficult to pronounce. Consequently, some students feel the need to change what they are called in the classroom. This immediately creates a feeling of unease or exclusion for the student. Learning an unfamiliar pronunciation is not difficult for students if taken one syllable at a time. As lead learner in a new classroom, the teacher can take the initiative to invite students to teach the community how to say their name correctly. In a cosmopolitan setting people may feel it is acceptable to say, "Oh my goodness, I will never be able to say your name properly. I'll just call you [*insert nickname here*]". No! It is important for everyone in the classroom community to understand that the first mark of respect for a person is knowing their preferred name and saying it correctly.

To set a model for inclusion in a classroom community, teachers may initiate some icebreaker activities such as sharing a personal characteristic or quality, then inviting students who wish to share to do likewise. For example, a teacher might begin with, "One thing about me is that I love taking learning outdoors, so I hope we can do a lot of that this year." Some students may be reticent but once the flow is going, it becomes an interesting exchange that quickly provides insights into what is important to community members. The sooner a teacher can get to know that one student loves writing but doesn't like to talk much, or that another is happiest working alone on the computer, the more quickly learning activities can be designed to meet the needs of all learners. A good opening topic is what hopes students have for the year, what they may be concerned about, or how they could help each other. Activities that begin to build relationships and community in the classroom, while also linking directly to curriculum, greatly assist in building community and launching learning.

Another popular activity across all grades and in teacher education is the use of glyphs. A glyph is a data management tool that allows students to display data pictorially. It can be adapted in complexity to suit any grade level. Students add symbols that represent personal information to a page or cutout shape. In the example below, the statement "My favorite sport is _____" allows students to participate in making a glyph whether they play the sport or enjoy watching it. Students may have physical limitations, financial constraints, or family responsibilities that prohibit participation in organized sports. Therefore, it is important to choose categories, and construct statements and prompts for conversation, that will ensure all students see themselves mirrored in the activity.

ACTION STRATEGY: GLYPHS

What…

A glyph is a visual representation of data. A legend allows students to create and read data included on a glyph. It can be used as a "get to know you" activity at the beginning of a new year, and also as a lesson to meet curricular outcomes in data management or geometric shapes.

For classroom implementation, a variety of colored stickers or shapes indicates different information. Younger students might have 3 or 4 categories per glyph. Older students can complete more complex glyphs. Glyphs can also be created using creative technology. Once glyphs are complete, students can analyze the data and sort it based on different criteria, adding grade-level-appropriate math calculations on ratios or percentages when analyzing the data. Students can also guess who created each glyph based on the data represented.

In this example from Kindergarten students, the glyph is in the shape of a fish. The students used the following legend to create a "story" about themselves. For young children the colors approximate the choice as much as possible (yellow = school bus, red = apple, and eyes are represented by their closest color). Glyphs can be sorted by one attribute to create groups, for example, all students who share the same favorite sport.

Shape	Meaning	Blue	Yellow	Green	Red	Brown
Eye	My eye color	Blue	—	Green	—	Brown
Circle	How I get to school	Walk	Bus	Car	Bicycle	—
Triangle	My favorite sport	Hockey	Soccer	Baseball	Football	—
Square	My favorite color	Blue	Yellow	Green	Red	Other
Rectangle	My favorite fruit	Berries	Banana	Pear	Apple	—

Implementation

How…

The class collaboratively creates a legend using symbols to include information that they would like to know about their classmates. Topics could include favorite sport, favorite animal, how I get to school, eye color, or other characteristic. (Teachers should be aware that categories must be inclusive to avoid marginalizing students. For example, it would be inappropriate to ask what type of home a student lives in.)

Each student uses the legend to create a glyph that represents their answers to the questions. Classmates can "read" each glyph to find information about the student who created it. Glyphs can be posted on a bulletin board and sorted by category (e.g. Everyone who walks to school).

Each day glyphs can be sorted using a different category. Once in groups, students can get to know each other using prompts such as, "What advice would we give to someone who wants to learn our favorite sport?" Prompts should elicit thinking that goes beyond simple information such as, "Why is _____ your favorite sport?" As students move into different groups based on the information on their glyph, they understand what they have in common with their classmates, and how they differ.

Why…

Glyphs provide students with an easy way to make connections and a fun way to get know each other. The complexity of the data can vary to make this activity accessible to very young students and the upper grades.

What If…

What if students did an activity with their "glyph group" (based on a single criterion) for the day to have an opportunity to get to know their classmates? What if the hockey group had to convince the baseball group and soccer group that their sport was the best? There are a lot of ways to engage students in community building through this activity, while learning data management skills.

Prior to developing the legend, consider how an activity might serve to invite a child's participation or to make them feel like an outsider in the environment. How might certain categories create discomfort or exclude some students?

In creating a classroom environment that respects each student, teachers must ensure that a seemingly simple activity does not leave a student feeling isolated from their peers. An example of this might be the traditional "back to school" story about their summer or spring vacation. While many students might have interesting stories to tell, others might have found a break from school to be challenging. The safety and security of the classroom may be a welcome relief for students after a difficult summer or spring break. Not every family can afford vacations and not all summer or vacation memories are good ones.

When choosing a topic for writing or conversation in the classroom, it is important to ensure that everyone has equal access. Consider using an imaginary character whose vacation children can creatively imagine, providing access for everyone. Students might write about Batman's vacation, or a place they might like to visit one day, or the story of a lost suitcase and where it ended up.

THROUGH THE WINDOW...

One year I received a betta fish as a gift from my family. I figured it would be more fun to keep it in the classroom than in my kitchen. So the fish and I went off to school. The students named him Happy. When it came time for spring break, my family and I were going to visit relatives in Canada's capital. Much to my family's dismay, I brought the fish home, covered the bowl with a shower cap, and brought Happy along on the car ride.

As we were traveling it hit me! How much fun would it be for the class to write about Happy's spring break? It seemed like a brilliant idea. My patient husband stopped as we approached the population sign for Canada's capital, Ottawa, for a photo op with Happy in front of the sign. Happy visited the parliament buildings, met a very gracious Royal Canadian Mounted Police Officer for another photo op, and even went to McDonald's for a Happy Meal.

Arriving back to school after spring break, I talked to the class about Happy's vacation and showed the photos. Soon, in small groups, we were writing a collaborative story that was full of much imagination. Each group wrote a page of the story. The students were so enthused by their work that we couldn't help but "publish" it using a discarded hardcover library book that we re-covered and decorated (see Action Strategy: Publishing, p. 92). Our school librarian catalogued our book and included it in the school collection. We even hosted a book launch in the library so other classes and teachers could "meet the authors", and Happy, who was proudly displayed on a pedestal (actually an upturned trash can covered in a cloth) in the library to greet visitors.

Much to my family's relief Happy did not accompany us on any other vacations, although Happy lived almost two years and started school again the following fall. Nevertheless, the learning that I gained from that experience about inclusion was huge. Taking a common activity, such as a "my vacation story" and turning it around so that everyone had access and could participate made for a rich learning experience for every student. There was great conversation about what each page of Happy's story would say, along with research into Canada's capital to provide accurate information. Our book launch in the library provided the students with opportunities to engage in authentic talk with other classes, teachers, and parents who came by to chat with the students about their experience as authors.

Thinking about inclusive practices in the classroom and the challenges students face before they even arrive at the classroom door, led me to create "Bricks in a Backpack" (Vetter in Cushner et al, 2014). This is an impactful "back to school" activity for teachers and in teacher education classrooms.

THROUGH THE WINDOW...

As an elementary classroom teacher, every Tuesday after Labour Day I watched the children arrive for the first time in my classroom. I noticed the bulging backpacks that each of them carried. Some backpacks were bright and new, sporting the logo of the latest cartoon character, sports team, or designer. Others were battered and worn. Every backpack contained a collection of items that were special to the owner. Some had a selection of pencils and markers. Some held a favorite toy. Most, but not all, held a lunch or snack for the day.

As I got to know my new students each year, I would begin to notice that in addition to their heavy backpacks many of my students carried other burdens to school each day. Although these burdens were invisible to the casual observer, their impact was great and served to marginalize the students who carried them in a multitude of ways.

Some students carried burdens of social weight—racism, bullying, poverty, broken homes, or abuse. Other students carried the weight of emotional or cognitive burdens—depression, issues of self-esteem, and learning challenges. Each of these burdens greatly influenced how a child learned, interacted, and engaged in the classroom.

Visualizing the invisible bricks in the backpacks of students helps teachers to empathize and to look beyond misbehaviors and/or academic struggles as they work to support all learners. As teachers, it is impossible for us to take on the burdens of every student, but we can raise our awareness and empathy for the struggles that many face. Many teachers carry burdens of their own. Many teachers come to the field having struggled in school and wanting to be, for another child, that caring teacher who supported and nurtured them years ago. Other teachers come to the field having experienced academic success in K–12 and university studies, accompanied by much pressure and stress to be the best. Regardless of our prior experience, we all carry the responsibility of ensuring that our classroom is a welcoming place where inclusion and equity are foundational to every class activity.

These experiences and many more have led me to engage in the practice of **turning to wonder** (Palmer, 2017) before acting. Turning to wonder sets my mind to asking why something is happening in my classroom. It is easy to rush to judgment. However, if we are to create a truly inclusive and equitable classroom, it is imperative to first turn to wonder: to wonder how our understanding or way of knowing and being in the world might be influencing our reactions and the reactions of students in our classrooms.

ACTION STRATEGY: TURNING TO WONDER

What...

Turning to Wonder instead of rushing to judgment is an ideal classroom strategy for use by teachers and by students. It is also a great strategy for life. When I walk through the mall parking lot and hear drivers exchanging heated and often foul language over a parking spot, I think how much better it would be for everyone if we all just turned to wonder far more often. Used in the classroom, Turning to Wonder encourages students and teachers to avoid judgment and consider understanding. Why did that student react in that manner? Why am I feeling hurt by that comment? Turning to Wonder diffuses anger and/or judgment and facilitates understanding and empathy.

Implementation

How...

This strategy is easy to implement but requires explicit teaching to ensure that students understand both the "how" and the "why" of Turning to Wonder. This is a perfect strategy to introduce through role play. Teachers can help students to learn the internal language that supports wondering, including phrases such as, "I wonder what the other person is feeling right now", or "I wonder if I am clearly understanding what the other person is saying", or "I wonder if there are other factors that are impacting this person or this conflict". When a member of the class, teacher or student, feels the urge to be angry or to judge, a conscious effort is made to stop, breathe, and turn to wonder through the engagement of an empathetic stance.

Why...

Too often classroom situations escalate unnecessarily when learning frustrations erupt into inappropriate behaviors. As a result, valuable learning time is lost to disruptions. Turning to wonder reminds students and teachers that while we may not have a choice as to another person's actions, we do have a choice in how we respond. Making a conscious effort to respond in a kind and empathetic manner improves the quality of life in the classroom for everyone.

What If...

What if turning to wonder became a strategy that applied not only to contentious interactions, but also to learning. What if we encouraged students to look at curriculum or learning challenges that might seem contentious as objects of wonder rather than frustration?

Teachers' days are busy. Curriculum puts many demands on classroom time. Often it can seem that one more thing to add to the day is simply one thing too many. Thinking of actions that enhance the equity and inclusivity of the classroom community as simply an alternative way of thinking about classroom practice, rather than an add-on to your daily tasks, creates a mindset for success.

As you implement a lesson plan that you have used before or set up your classroom for a new day, term, or year, allow yourself a moment to turn to wonder… to wonder how you might tweak just one little thing in that lesson that might make a difference to a child. After a while, all those little tweaks will move your classroom toward your visualization of a true classroom community. Every positive step takes us closer!

Mentoring Partnerships within the Community

Through my work at a faculty of education with both community organization-based practicum experiences and school-based teaching experiences I was responsible for thousands of mentoring partnerships. In our university, practicum experiences were centrally arranged. This meant that students were assigned placements. They did not choose their own host classroom with a mentoring partner who they knew would share their philosophies or priorities. Making mentoring partnerships work between often very different people was the objective of each day.

Although the use of terminology such as host teacher or associate teacher is common in our area, we chose to refer to the teachers who welcomed teacher candidates into their classrooms as **mentor teachers**. For us, this distinction was important. We believed that mentor teachers did more than act as a host to a teacher candidate and more than simply act as an associate. The teachers who welcomed our university's teacher candidates were, indeed, mentors. We saw the role as a partnership. Generally, the mentor teacher brought classroom and/or field experience, while the teacher candidate brought life experience, along with talents and skills, that enhanced the partnership. Often in a time of rapidly changing technology, many teacher candidates were able to share skills related to digital technology. Others came with backgrounds in the arts or working with special needs students. Therefore the concept of a **mentoring partnership** fit well with our understanding of what was actually happening in classrooms.

During the research for a study on mentoring, my research partners and I heard from teachers that many of the strategies we were advocating between mentor teacher and teacher candidate to develop professional relationships were working for them in building classroom communities, too. One of the teachers in the study said, "I could do that with my kids. How awesome would that be? Transferable stuff" (Parker and Vetter, 2020). While one may traditionally think of a mentor as a more knowledgeable other, within the classroom environment students have the capacity to mentor other students in a variety of ways and in fluid partnerships that leverage the experiences and understandings of both partners.

Mentoring relationships in a classroom of students differs from that of a one-on-one mentoring relationship that takes place between adults in a professional setting. Within a classroom community, a student may be a mentor to many students on one topic and be mentored by a variety of students in other ways. As a result, mentoring partnerships in classroom communities must be flexible and responsive to the needs of each student and the availability of mentorship by others. At times mentoring may be a "one-off" experience. At other times, it may be an ongoing process. Students may know each other well from prior grades or years at the school and have developed friendships that also serve as mentoring partnerships extending from year to year. In other cases, students may find themselves increasingly isolated or excluded from the community when opportunities to form learning or mentoring partnerships have not arisen.

So I asked this question:

For detailed discussion of teachers mentoring each other, please see *Mentoring Each Other: Teachers Listening, Learning and Sharing to Create More Successful Classrooms.*
— (Parker and Vetter, 2020).

How might we facilitate flexible peer-mentoring partnerships to build community and support student learning?

I recall an example from an upper elementary classroom. There was a student in my class who interacted less with the other students. He loved to be on the computer and rarely participated in playground games. He was often the victim of playground teasing. Of course, this rankled me, but I needed to find a way to deal with the situation without directly intervening.

> **THROUGH THE WINDOW...**
>
> Using the strategy of modeling what I wanted to see in the classroom, I began to ask the student to help me when a computer issue arose. He was always eager to help and had developed sound understandings of how to use the various software programs that were available in our school. I did not contrive ways to involve the student, rather I took advantage of his expertise when I might normally go through a series of trial-and-error moves to resolve a computer problem. Before long other students in the classroom took note. When an issue arose, they would ask if he could help them. He loved the opportunity to do so, and as he did, his expertise grew and so did his self-esteem. His involvement with students' computer issues also engaged him in conversations about topics students were researching and expanded his confidence in joining in during group discussions and classroom conversations.
>
> When the librarian buzzed our classroom one day to ask if he could come to the library to help with a particular issue, his reputation soared and I had to gently set a limit on the amount of time he would spend as our computer guru. It was a great opportunity for our class to discuss the importance of enhancing their own computer skills, rather than relying solely on their new mentor. We managed to find a balance and the year ended successfully for the student and for our classroom community who had now embraced a student who had previously been on the fringe of social interactions.

In isolation, this example is simply a heartwarming story, but every teacher has a personal library of such stories that they could share. Perhaps you might look into your own library of classroom stories to seek examples of how and when your students took it upon themselves to mentor each other. In doing so I invite you to turn to wonder, asking:

- What might I have learned from my personal story that would encourage me to create more opportunities for students mentoring students in my classroom?
- What activities might I facilitate to encourage students to move beyond sharing information in group projects and become co-creators of new learning and deeper understandings?
- How might I reinforce student behaviors that facilitate students mentoring students?
- How might I model for students the value of shared experience and discovery through collaboration and communication?

Mentoring partnerships provide students with understandings that friends and mentoring partners can disagree about and discuss collaboratively when opinions differ. Learning to support and accept support and consider different opinions from peers is a valuable life skill.

In all elementary grades, investigation of social issues that impact the school community allows the students to come together, share opinions, develop awareness of alternate perspectives, deepen thinking, and enhance communication skills. With a collaborative objective of creating an authentic, relevant, meaningful, and purposeful project, students learn to focus on the collective outcome. Differences are more easily resolved when there is a common goal in mind. One such activity is podcasting, where students get involved in collaboratively researching and recording their learning for use by others and by the parent community on a secured school website.

Podcasts allow students to articulate their perspectives to an authentic audience. Many school districts have websites where students and parents can securely access student-created recordings. In some classrooms, shared files in an offline folder allow students to listen to each other's podcasts and follow up with community conversations. Students working collaboratively on podcasts dig deeper as they challenge and build upon each other's thinking, opinions, and facts to be included in the podcast. The depth of the research and the level of thinking for all students increases. It is easy to spout off an opinion; however, the responsibility to justify that opinion with accurate information in a format that is respectful and appropriate for access by peers (and parents) requires careful planning, consideration, and production. As students share their understandings and opinions, they are required to analyze and evaluate, then build new ideas and concepts, based on the collaboration.

ACTION STRATEGY: PODCASTS

What...

Creating podcasts gives voice to student ideas, concerns, and perspectives. Within the safety of a classroom-controlled website, students have the opportunity to reach an authentic audience that is determined by the teacher and/or the school district, sharing their carefully researched and considered opinions on current topics that relate to classroom conversations and/or curriculum. Students become aware of the power of words to influence, recognizing that what they read and listen to also has the power to influence their thinking. Podcasting also supports students' sense of responsibility by reminding them that their words have the potential to go beyond the classroom.

Implementation

How...

Topics related to curriculum, student readings, student interest, and more become launching pads for inquiry, planning, and recording of podcasts. A secure school district-approved site that allows students to broadcast to an authentic yet safely controlled audience provides students with motivation to make their voices heard. If a secure site is not available, podcasts can be saved and accessed by peers on classroom computers only. Students research and plan their topics individually or as a group. Prior to recording, students ensure that their information is accurate, consider their audience to ensure appropriate content, tone, and language, and develop an awareness of alternate perspectives that may challenge the content of their podcast.

Why...

21st-century technology allows everyone to broadcast their views on any topic. Facilitating student awareness of the impact that their voice may have on others is crucial. What a student posts in 2023 will continue to reside in cyberspace for many years. Providing students with understandings of the importance of considering what they post and how they express their opinions and perspectives will serve them well into the future.

What If...

My father always said that you can't put old heads on young shoulders. This is so true for today's students whose TikTok or Instagram posts may come back to haunt them years from now. What if our students could develop an awareness today of their digital impact on tomorrow, and on their future lives? This can only happen if teachers engage in open and respectful conversations with students and take initiative to make explicit to students their responsibility to post wisely.

Students working together to dig into an issue that is important to them have the opportunity move beyond sharing understandings. Within student-to-student mentoring partnerships, they create new understandings, develop higher-level thinking, and launch new wonderings that spur future learning.

I began this section with a description of teachers mentoring other teachers and noted the importance of explicitly using the term "mentor". Such explicit naming of students as mentors is also an important action in the classroom setting where students are mentoring other students. When students hear themselves referred to as mentors and understand their role of mentor as a thinker who guides another, they put greater weight on their actions as they engage with their peers. The sense of being responsible for their own learning *and* for that of a classmate increases the perceived value of the work they are doing. Naming and recognizing the role of mentoring within the classroom creates a greater sense of belonging as students become invested in their own success and that of their peers.

The mentoring community becomes stronger through the common objective of increasing everyone's opportunity to achieve. And the opportunity for everyone to achieve increases greatly when all are supported by a strong community. The result is a growing momentum that builds community relationships and underpins student success.

3

Realities of the Classroom

I was recently invited to share my thoughts on classroom talk for an education blog being launched by a provincial government (Quebec Education, 2022). I immediately recalled my experience teaching grade 5. I had taught the other grades in the primary and junior divisions including split classrooms. However, this would be my first time in a grade 5 classroom. I was very excited to have the opportunity.

I have always found that teaching a new grade or course is inspiring. It helps to get me thinking about new and different ways of delivering curriculum and facilitating learning for the students. My father used to say that "A change is as good as a rest." I was intending to make this expression come to life and let the new space enliven my teaching.

I was assigned a portable classroom at the far end of the schoolyard, which, at first, seemed like a great opportunity. Beyond the walls of the school building, with direct access to the schoolyard, I imagined that our learning might also be "portable". In other words, we could take it outdoors and expand our horizons, both literally and figuratively. As the end of summer approached, I began to make my plans for our new "home". I was full of excitement about working with the grade 5 class and creating a rich talk, collaborative learning community.

Then I walked into that space. It was a *box*…a rectangular box with windows on one side, blackboards at the front, coat racks at the back and a side wall with faded bulletin boards. Thinking outside the portable classroom *box* would definitely be required. The portable seemed much smaller than other classrooms that I had been in. Absolutely full to the rafters of "stuff", it seemed almost claustrophobic.

I must admit that I am a low-clutter person at the best of times, but walking into that classroom sent my head spinning. There were so many desks and chairs, bookshelves, textbooks, bits and pieces, bulletin boards with faded maps, and bins full of who knows what. I tried to imagine where I could find a place to put a pencil or find a space to think. In my mind having a space to think means having room to move and to breathe in an environment whose openness invites similarly open thinking. To say the least, it was discouraging. The dream of developing collaborative learning, creating community, and facilitating authentic, relevant, meaningful, and purposeful talk in this space seemed to get lost in clutter.

Much to the dismay of other teachers and, no doubt, the principal, I began to move much of the "stuff" from my portable into the storage room. I even exchanged my teacher's desk, which was a very large and cumbersome piece, for a small table. Then I removed every possible bit of clutter. I was ruthless in discarding resources that were outdated. If my students were to become 21st-century thinkers, they could not do so with inaccurate information about a rapidly changing world. As I emptied bookcases and shelves, the space began to grow.

Originally, the student desks were in rows that filled the limited floor space. I pushed all the student desks against the walls in groups of four. This allowed me to create an empty space in the centre of the room. I made sure to turn the desk compartments to the inside so they couldn't be used to store forgotten lunches and assorted junk. In the centre of each group, I placed a communal basket to keep pens, pencils, erasers, scissors, glue sticks, etc. Textbooks and notebooks were stored in milk-type crates on shelves and could be easily accessed as required.

I added a small, low, round table in the centre of the space with a blue cloth and a little vase of polyester flowers.

As the term progressed, that table and that space became our little oasis. The students would bring their chairs and create a circle around the table. At first it was a bit chaotic as twenty-eight kids dragged chairs and jostled for position in the circle. But perseverance paid off and soon students realized sitting beside someone other than their best friend made a nice change, and it wasn't a problem to lift one's chair rather than drag it across the floor.

We came to that circle every day at the end of class to share the best and the most challenging parts of our day, or a poem that someone felt everyone would enjoy, or to talk about an event in the news. We came to the circle to hear the salient points of a lesson or topic of discussion before returning to the groups for focused conversation and discovery. We used the circle as a place to solve problems and to reflect quietly as a community when things went wrong. The table held a variety of items that came and went… a scarlet leaf from a maple tree, an oddly shaped rock, and whatever seemed to add a sense of peace to our space.

When I reflect on that time and space, I no longer see size or "stuff". I hear voices sharing stories, points of view, concerns, perspectives, learnings, and laughter. I feel the problems and the peace that we brought to our circle for sharing and resolution.

As a teacher/researcher I would have loved to examine in detail the conversations that took place in that classroom, the sense of community that pervaded the space, and the collaborative spirit that students embraced. Unfortunately, the challenge of taking on a new grade in a new environment were sufficient to keep me busy. However, as a keen observer of students and their learning, I could definitely see that the opportunity to think outside the "box" of our portable classroom made for a unique learning experience. I am left to wonder if the talk created our community or if the community that we created was the catalyst for the collaboration and rich talk that engaged us in our daily learning.

Setting the Stage for Talk, Collaboration, and Community

The problem with schooling is that we have so little time to experiment in *getting it right*. What does *getting it right* even mean? Surely it is different for every teacher and for every group of students as classroom dynamics change.

Students arrive for the new academic year in a classroom that has been organized for them by their teacher. There is much work to be done and curriculum to be covered. Before we know it, Thanksgiving is upon us. We may tweak a few things, but time is marching on and there is just so much to be done. How do we find the time to experiment with new ideas and make changes in a busy classroom environment?

As you read through this chapter, I hope you will be kind to yourself. Sift through the information to find one or two nuggets of gold that you might be able to use in your classroom. It is unrealistic to think that you will revamp your entire classroom and your students will arrive on Monday morning to a whole new environment. For many students it would be highly unsettling. If you do consider a major change, give the students a heads-up before they leave on Friday. Explain what changes you are making and how it will make the classroom a better place for everyone.

Remember there are always small changes that can be easily implemented. A few minor changes here and there as the year progresses can make a big difference. And if the minor adjustments you make don't suit your needs after a reasonable trial period, it is not a huge challenge to try something else. So open your mind and your classroom to a few new ideas.

The Physical Environment

The objective in designing the physical environment of the classroom is to create an inviting and inclusive space where every student feels that they belong. It is not simply about removing clutter and making space for community circles around a little table that acts as a central focus. An effective physical environment mirrors your philosophy of teaching and learning, and the faces, interests, and realities of all of the children in the classroom.

So I asked this question:

How might the intentional act of creating a community-centred physical space build relationships and facilitate collaborative learning and communication?

The action of moving desks to the perimeter of the classroom is the first big step in moving to a community-centred physical space. Groups of four desks can be positioned tight against the walls to open up a gathering space in the centre of the room. The desks basically circle the room, although certain areas may require open space to access shelves. If this is not practical, then a horseshoe setup or two parallel lines of four-desk groups along each outer wall also works well. The teacher's space forms part of the circular arrangement. There is no "front" of the classroom, although blackboard or interactive white board (IWB) placement may require open access for a small group to gather with or without teacher support.

A key priority in a central focus design is the use of a student-centred approach with the teacher and students collaborating in the learning. Direct instruction where the teacher stands at a blackboard or IWB is replaced by student-centred learning with the teacher serving as coach, collaborator, facilitator, or lead learner who joins small groups of students as required. Whole class meetings or sharing sessions take place in the open space at the centre of the room. A small table acts as a focal point in the centre of the room.

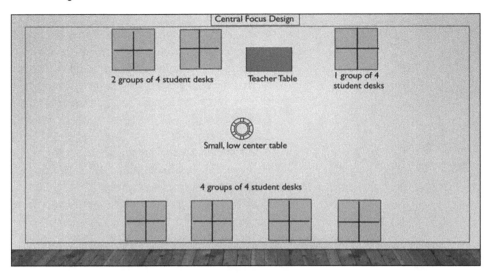

When it is time to come to the circle, students are invited to carry (not drag) their chairs to form a circle around the small table. For a brief gathering, students can stand in the circle.

ACTION STRATEGY: CENTRAL FOCUS DESIGN

What...

Central Focus Design is a classroom layout strategy that moves desks toward the outer edges of the room leaving a centre space open to allow the class to gather in a circle for whole class discussions and meetings. Within the central area, a small table acts as a focal point and may serve as a repository for items that are meaningful to the community. Students can focus or reflect on the items while restoring a sense of calm or academic concentration. Students can come to the central circle with their chairs or sit on the floor. Moving chairs to the circle quickly and quietly soon becomes routine.

Implementation

How...

Student desks are moved to the outer edges of the room in groups of four. A circular or U-shape layout, or parallel lines along outer walls, include a teacher's table. Desk storage compartments are turned inward. Students' backpacks hang on backs of chairs or on cloakroom hooks. Group seating may be assigned for specific tasks, freely chosen for others, or randomly assigned (see Action Strategy: Playing Card Groups, p. 56). The central area becomes a sharing circle, where students gather as a community to learn, share ideas, and resolve community concerns. Moving to a central focus design is best undertaken prior to the first day of class in a new academic year, or at a mid-term break. A mid-term reset of the classroom layout/routine may be unsettling to some students; therefore, the teacher should explain the "what, how, why, and what if" of central focus design prior to students arrival. Notebooks and texts are stored in labelled crates or baskets on shelves for easy access, and are retrieved by one student per group, as required.

The four-desk groups make for a symmetrical space. Some groups may only have three members due to the class size not being divisible by four. If space permits, one or two desks can be set up as independent study spots, similar to a library study carrel. The teacher's desk being part of the circular arrangement creates a physical sense of equity in the classroom. While it is understood that the teacher has ultimate responsibility for the classroom, the role of teacher as a *partner* in learning is emphasized by the placement of the teacher's space within the classroom layout.

The question often arises of how to manage with a teacher's *table* and no drawers. Frankly, it becomes quite liberating not to have drawers full of junk. Like the students, the teacher's table has a basket for pens, scissors, and assorted bits and pieces, along with a tape dispenser and stapler. A lunch stored in the staffroom fridge requires the teacher to get out of the classroom and socialize, or take a walk for a breath of fresh air while students are at recess. A small box under the desk can hold a purse or other personal item out of sight.

THROUGH THE WINDOW…

In my grade 5 portable classroom, my coat and boots hung alongside the students' outerwear. Frankly that was the only place for my things, but it also allowed me to model for students that if I took a moment to securely hang my coat on a hook and put my boots side by side, my coat would not be in a wet lump on the floor and my boots would not be separated from each other when it was time to go outdoors. Clearly, this was not an overnight miracle. However, sending students back to pick up coats and set boots side by side soon convinced them that doing it right the first time was the easiest method.

In a central focus design classroom, existing bookshelves can be used to hold milk-style plastic crates. Each crate is labeled to contain texts (math, science, social studies) or notebooks divided by subject. At the beginning of a lesson, one student per group goes to the crates to retrieve the required notebooks or textbooks for their group. In a classroom of twenty-eight students, this means only seven students are out of their seats when it is time to retrieve books or replace them in crates. To review student notebooks, the appropriate crate can simply be lifted to the teacher's table. This eliminates the need to collect notebooks or go looking for them in messy desks. With the implementation of carefully curated digital media and websites by education publishers as resources, complemented by peer mentors who act as catalysts for questioning, wondering, and inquiry, the collection of hardcover texts can be shared.

The book crates also address another issue in the classroom — the seating plan. With all texts and notebooks in crates on the bookshelves, there is no need for students to have assigned seating. All desks are turned with the storage compartments to the centre so they are not accessible. There is always room between groups to allow each student to hang their backpack on their chair to hold any personal belongings. Ideally, tables instead of desks work best for flexible groupings; however, groups of four desks also work well.

It is no secret that students generally want to sit with their friends. At a teachers' workshop, it is no different. We like to sit with our friends, too. However, if the objective is to form a classroom community, it is important for students to get to know everyone in the classroom. They will not all be the best of friends, but they need to know how to collaborate with others who have different learning styles, interests, and abilities. Teamwork and collaborative skills are high on the list of competencies that 21st-century employers are seeking.

With seating unassigned, students have the opportunity to sit with their "working group" for specific projects. At other times students simply choose a random seat. To ensure that students have the opportunity to work with different people, they can move to "playing card groups". The teacher may choose to preplan the "playing card groups" or simply distribute playing cards randomly as students enter. Everyone who gets a number 4, for example, is required to sit in group 4, and so on. Providing this flexible grouping allows students to get to know everyone well and learn to work with learners who have different learning styles and/or levels. Initially, students may be reluctant to move to a playing card group, but the mix of flexible and assigned groupings soon becomes a matter of routine and is often a welcome change for students, many of whom do not want to work with the same peers all the time.

ACTION STRATEGY: PLAYING CARD GROUPS

What...

This simple strategy provides the opportunity to change student work groups in keeping with a preset plan, or randomly as students enter the classroom. A simple deck of playing cards allows the teacher to hand out a card to each student. The total number of cards corresponds to the number of students in the classroom — for example, 28 students = 7 groups of 4. Therefore use all 4 card suits from Ace to 7. The students sit at the group indicated by the number on their playing card. The selection may be totally random or pre-selected by the teacher. The key is to retrieve the cards once everyone is seated so the deck is ready for subsequent use.

Implementation

How...

Ensure each table, or group of desks, is labelled with a number (28 students = 7 groups of 4; 25 students = 4 groups of 4 and 3 groups of 3). The configuration will change with class size; however, each group should have a minimum of 3 members and a maximum of 4. Using a deck of standard playing cards, the teacher uses cards Ace to 7 to assign groups. Students who receive a number 4 upon entry sit at group 4. If you will have one or more groups of 3, remember to remove the 4th card for that group number before distributing the cards. Teachers can preplan groups by handing out the appropriate card to specific students according to the plan. At first, students may be reticent to sit with classmates they do not know well. However, they soon become accustomed to collaborating with a variety of classmates. Groups can change by time slot (morning, after recess, lunch, after gym class, etc.), or by curriculum activity (science group, math group, etc.). It is important to ensure desk compartments are turned inwards to avoid having students leave personal items or food behind when they change groups. Backpacks can hang on the backs of chairs or on a cloakroom hook. Be sure to collect cards when groups are seated so they are ready for use again. Initially some students may try to trade cards to sit with a friend, but soon they will come to appreciate the system as their "friend group" increases to include everyone in the class.

Why...

21st-century research lists teamwork as a key competency for success in the workplace. Developing skills to work collaboratively and communicate effectively with a variety of peers is a life skill that will serve students well in the future. In a world of rapidly changing technologies and work environments, the ability to adapt to change is of great value.

What If...

What if students were supported in developing understandings that everyone brings unique skills, understandings and aptitudes to a group project. Learning to appreciate the skills of all group members and accept diverse perspectives enriches learning. (See Action Strategy: What I Bring, p. 26)

In terms of teacher organization, lesson plans, materials, and required resources can also be kept in a basket on a bookshelf. With five labeled baskets on the bookshelf (Monday, Tuesday, Wednesday, Thursday, and Friday), if a lesson is not completed, or scheduling of a special event or assembly means that a lesson needs to be moved to the following day, then the content for that lesson is simply transferred to the next day's basket. If a supply teacher is coming to the classroom, everything is readily available in the appropriate day's basket. This makes classroom organization particularly simple. If there is something that is going to be needed for Friday's lesson, it can be tossed in the Friday basket at any time during the week. After school each day, the basket for the next day is checked by the teacher to make sure all is in order and, if not, materials can be sourced so the teacher (or a supply teacher) has everything at hand when it is time to implement the lesson.

While some readers may be marveling at these organizational skills, others will have uncovered the truth. I am often disorganized, then find myself frazzled when I have to scramble as the day is about to begin. This strategy saves time, spares frazzled nerves, and ensures I have everything I need for the day in one place.

ACTION STRATEGY: LESSON BASKETS

What…

A basket or plastic bin labeled for each day of the week is placed on a shelf easily accessible to the teacher's desk. Items needed for a lesson are put in the appropriate basket prior to the teaching day. Changes simply mean moving items from the Monday basket to the Tuesday basket, etc., as required. When an unexpected absence occurs materials are ready for a substitute or occasional teacher. For the classroom teacher, morning arrival is less stressed if lesson baskets are waiting.

Implementation

How…

The first step is a visit to the local dollar store for 5 baskets or boxes that fit on your classroom shelves and will hold what you typically need for a day of teaching. Generally a basket that allows an 8½" x 11" piece of paper to lie flat is a good size. Label each basket for a day of the week. The prior teaching day, toss whatever will be needed for the next day into the basket. If a lesson was not completed on a day as planned, simply move the items for that lesson into the next day's basket. If lesson plans are generally printed, then a copy of the lesson plan can be included in the daily basket. If lesson plans are online, a simple note at the bottom of the online plan can indicate "See Monday Basket" to locate the required resources. The basket might include samples of and/or materials for an art activity, photocopies required for student handouts, attendance records, reminder sticky notes, a list of focal students for daily assessment, read-aloud texts, and more.

Why…

Life is stressful. For many teachers, arrival at school happens after getting their own kids ready for the day, packing lunches, and racing out the door. Walking into the classroom to find what you need ready and waiting allows for a few minutes to catch your breath and start off with a calmer state of mind. A lesson basket for the day is also a visual reminder of what is on today's "to do" list — "Oh yeah, I have to send the permission slips home today" — and if you forget, they can be moved to tomorrow's basket.

What If…

What if you took time to look at your classroom to figure out what would make your life easier and more manageable? Is there clutter from prior years and/or prior teachers that intrudes on your space and your mind? What simple changes will make your life less stressful? Lesson baskets may not work for you, but stopping to consider how we can organize our teaching days and our space to reduce stress and increase a sense of calm in the classroom is time well invested.

One vital aspect of the physical organization of the classroom is the central focus table. The table is a space that represents what is in the collective hearts and minds of the students. An initial vase of polyester flowers might remain as a symbol of serenity or be replaced by a clear bowl of fall leaves or a collection of canned goods for a Thanksgiving food drive. A small pair of children's shoes might rest on the table to support reflection on the National Day for Truth and Reconciliation. Other items that grace the table may reflect the changing seasons or the curriculum focus of the classroom.

In the busy-ness of a classroom, it is unrealistic to think that every student (and teacher) is focused on the learning 100 percent of the time. We all need those moments to briefly escape into our thoughts and return refreshed to the learning. The central focus table can serve as a place to direct our gaze when students or teacher need a mental break away from the work of the day.

The key element of a physical classroom layout with central focus design is the opportunity to come together as community.

THROUGH THE WINDOW...

Twenty minutes prior to the final bell, the students gathered in a circle around the centre table to focus on each other and the work of the day. Sometimes the discussion highlighted challenges in the learning and how the students might move beyond those challenges. Other times, the focus was on an issue of classroom dynamics, a concern or problem that needed to be addressed. Yet other times, students wanted to share personal concerns (e.g. "Today was a difficult day because…") that alerted students and teacher to a need to be empathetic about a specific situation. Sometimes a poem, quote, or song that resonated with the group was shared and reflected upon. And sometimes students just sat quietly, breathed deeply, and engaged in a few moments of calm after a busy day. Often students took the opportunity to show appreciation during this time for something another student had done to support their learning or to make their day a little brighter. When the bell rang, students were still eager to get home, but the race to the door slowed, perhaps imitating the reflective nature of the final daily circle.

In today's classrooms that have been greatly impacted by a global pandemic and a trend in the acceptability of negative commentary in online platforms, appreciations become a valuable aspect of community building (Gibbs, 1987).

ACTION STRATEGY: APPRECIATIONS

What…

This strategy has become a standard in many classrooms. It involves taking the time to articulate appreciation for the contributions of other members of the classroom community. Using the Action Strategy: Central Focus Design (see p. 54) to establish a gathering place within the classroom, it becomes easy to meet as a class and end the day on a positive note by considering what students are grateful for during the school day, within the community, and in their personal lives.

In busy classrooms, small kindnesses are often overlooked. Taking time to offer appreciations serves two purposes. It recognizes what individuals do to support the classroom community and it makes apparent to those who are less inclined to support others that small kindnesses are noticed and appreciated.

Implementation

How...

The implementation of this strategy begins with modeling by the teacher. The teacher ends the day by thanking the students for something in particular that happened that day. For example, "I really appreciate that you collaborated with each other so well today. I know our new science work is challenging, but everyone helped each other to understand and participate. So, thank you! Does anyone else want to tell us what they appreciate about our day?" In the beginning students may choose not to participate, or there may be repetitions in what they have to say. Any new process takes time to embed itself into the classroom dynamic. Appreciations can also happen throughout the day by speaking directly to one student and expressing appreciation for an act of kindness. It is important to be sincere in the appreciations to ensure that they are heartfelt and not simply glib statements.

Why...

As noted in other strategies, classrooms that function as a community achieve much greater success. The harmony created by a close community reduces behaviors that interrupt learning and facilitates collaboration and celebration of community achievements. Time lost to off-task or disruptive issues is significantly reduced when the overall learning environment recognizes the value of each individual member.

What If...

What if students and teachers used the open expression of appreciation in the classroom to establish harmonious relationships and create an environment where students feel safe in sharing their thoughts or dissenting opinions? "You and I have different perspectives on cell phones in the classroom, but I appreciate your honesty in sharing your thinking."

To ensure the sincerity of the expression, not every student is expected to voice an appreciation every day. However, a few simple and heartfelt public appreciations in the circle end the day on a positive note.

The classroom circle is not only for use at the end of the day. It can also be a whole-class jumping-off point for small group or independent inquiry. Listening to each other and considering alternative opinions in circle conversations allows students to reflect on their own thinking and, often, re-evaluate premature judgments. Importantly, circle conversations help students to clarify their current thinking and develop the wonderings that will take them deeper into subsequent learning. When students come to understand that the circle is designed as a place for their voices to be heard, they value the time in the circle and the voices shared.

The final aspect of the physical make-up of the classroom reflects the resources and visual contents of bulletin boards. In the democratic spirit of a central focus classroom, students lead the creation of bulletin boards to highlight themes that emerge from their learning (see Action Strategy: Thinking Journeys, p. 113) or special celebrations of classroom work.

It is always important to reflect student interests and experiences. A classroom reading basket full of texts that students select to share with classmates (either brought from home or signed out of the library) adds appeal to taking some independent reading time after lunch. The reading basket is always subject to the students' curate-and-critique process (see Action Strategy: Curate and Critique, p. 20). In an equitable and inclusive environment, the reading basket should reflect content that is respectful of everyone in the classroom. Any texts that arrive in the classroom for read-aloud, research, or textbook study invite consideration of voice, message, and veracity.

Looking holistically at the physical space of central focus design, a few points are worth emphasizing.

✓ The physical environment reflects the students in the classroom, their interests, and their individuality in learning.
✓ The ownership of and responsibility for the creation and maintenance of an equitable and inclusive environment is shared collaboratively by both students and teacher.
✓ The experience of working collaboratively with multiple groups and learning partners supports students in building a cohesive classroom community.
✓ The opportunity to have their voices heard in the classroom circle demonstrates to students that they belong in the environment and potentially mitigates behaviors that disrupt the community as a whole.
✓ The willingness of the teacher to share responsibility with the students for learning, communication, and community-building impacts the overall functioning of the classroom environment.

When students are given the time to communicate and collaborate in community, the learning is richer and deeper for all. Having the opportunity to work with a variety of peers provides students with a window into how others problem-solve, communicate, and think about the world. Student engagement in the learning of the classroom improves as students see learning through the perspectives of others. Importantly, students see themselves as valuable and valued members of the community.

Technology and Community

While there is much evidence that the use of technology in 21st-century classrooms has the potential to enhance student learning and produce more successful classrooms, it cannot be presumed that simply introducing technology into a classroom will reap learning rewards.

Teachers who successfully integrate technology into their classrooms understand fully that while technology is a wonderful tool for learning, it is not in itself the pedagogy. Technology is like a piece of chalk, another tool that continues to be used in classrooms around the world. The tool can be helpful but it is only as effective as the person wielding it.

So I asked this question:

How might collaborative learning through technology be effectively integrated into the pedagogy of a classroom community?

As I began my inquiry into technology in the classroom, it was important to recognize that technology is not readily available in every classroom. Many communities have limited budgets for technology and challenges with internet connections due to lack of local infrastructure and/or weather. In addition, the prior knowledge that students bring regarding the use of technology for learning is often closely linked to access, which is not equitable across school districts.

Technology is quickly changing and funding in most school districts does not stretch to include constant updates. In many communities, funding for technology in the school may be supported through fundraising by parent committees, yet again the inequity is apparent when the demographics of a school community do not support significant fundraising.

Today's range of technology and innovative devices makes it impractical to engage in a prescriptive conversation about classroom technology. Indeed, the discussion of implementing specific equipment, applications, websites, or learning platforms is beyond the scope of this book. Therefore this section looks at the overarching considerations of technology in a collaborative classroom environment, including:

- assessing and evaluating digital resources;
- developing an online instructional space;
- supporting equitable learning; and
- technology and the community.

Digital Resources

To assess and evaluate digital resources, it is helpful to think about how you might choose a non-digital resource. Perhaps review the Curate-and-Critique Action Strategy (see p. 20), which provides basic guidelines applicable across all media. Students should also be encouraged to add to computer folders or hard copy journals that review technology available to them in the classroom. A simple rating system with a comment ensures that students realize their personal responsibility in curating and critiquing what they see on the screen.

Students and teachers need to ask what is emphasized in the content and what is missing, then whose voice is heard in the narrative and whose is excluded. It is unrealistic to think that anything we view or read is totally neutral or factual. The inclusion of certain facts on a topic and the exclusion of others depends on the lens of the author or creator of the content. For example, two resources on the weather in my town might include daily average temperatures. However, a site with an environmental lens might focus on facts about the impact of weather on land erosion, water quality, and wildlife, while a site with a commercial lens might focus on facts about most favorable times to access tourist attractions. Any evaluation of these two sites would be based on the needs of the viewer. Therefore the question becomes, "Does the resource meet the learning needs of the students?"

Teachers need to consider if a site upholds their pedagogical stance. For example, I would lean towards a site that provides students with opportunities to respond, record, and self-assess their learning. Questions I'd ask would include:

- What is the main value of the site to learners?
- Does this resource provide information/teach in a manner that is appropriate for students in my classroom?
- Does the site consider multiple perspectives on a topic and help students to develop their own thinking?
- Who funds the site or controls the information? What agenda might be associated with that funding?
- What advertising is visible on the webpage? Is the advertising appropriate for student viewing?

Access that is equitable for all students in the classroom is a most important consideration in choosing a new resource. A few questions to ask yourself:

- Do students need a specific device to access the resource? If so, is that device available to all?
- Is the language appropriate in level for all learners?
- Do all the students see themselves reflected in the content of the resource?
- Does the resource allow students to engage at multiple levels?
- In what ways might this resource enhance the thinking and learning of all students?
- How might this resource support student learning beyond the traditional lesson?
- How might this resource increase or limit opportunities for student interaction, collaboration, and communication?
- How might this resource support inclusion and community connections within the classroom community?
- Does this resource invite families to share in the learning with their children?
- Do students have the technical expertise to effectively navigate and explore the resource?

Questioning the value of a specific technology or web resource ensures that student time and school funding is well invested in appropriate resources. It also helps teachers to understand the skills development that might be required to ensure all students are competent users and have access to the online learning supported in the classroom.

Developing an Online Instructional Space

Having the opportunity to develop an online instructional space is of great value to many teachers, students, and their families. Opportunities within such a space include a folder where teachers can create direct instructional segments of a curriculum-based lesson or remedial supports for students who need to review prior learning before accessing new content. Students who need more time to process direct instruction can view, pause, and review the recorded direct instruction segments as often as necessary to suit their learning needs.

Teachers can also record various "how to…" segments that students can access before beginning a new project. For example, a teacher might record a "How to Search the Internet" segment, or any number of brief video segments describing how to create a podcast, a slide or video presentation, or a blog. While some students may be independent users of technology, the "how to" segments are of great value to those who are less skilled in the use of technology.

It is important to look at how your students will access the learning in your online instructional space.

- Is it easy for students to find what they are looking for?
- Are there visual cues for students whose reading skills may not include deciphering complex instructions?
- Will students be able to navigate the site independently, clicking the correct links to find where they need to be to complete an activity?
- How might the site lessen or contribute to the stress of learning?

Online instructional spaces are also useful for parent access. Background information on what students are learning can be accessible to parents who want to help with their child's homework. Being able to access classroom learning information and protocols ensures that parents and students are on the same page when it comes to classroom learning and activities. However, it is also important to recognize that not all parents have the technology at home or the time available to delve into a classroom portal. It is important not to have expectations for parent participation that further excludes or marginalizes students when parents are unable to support the learning.

It may seem that an online instructional space shared with parents might become an additional burden for the teacher. However, teachers who provide a window into classroom activity through an online instructional site often find that the need for ongoing back-and-forth with parents lessens. In addition, the understanding that teachers, parents, and students are members of a three-way partnership in the space seems to encourage students to take greater ownership of their responsibility for classroom learning. When students see their parents as engaged members of the classroom community they develop greater appreciation for the supports available and the value that everyone places on successful learning.

An important aspect of the online instructional space is the time that it saves in the classroom, time that can be dedicated to personal interactions with students. When direct instruction is provided by video, classroom time is dedicated to active and collaborative problem-solving between students with teacher support. Although this strategy may seem best suited to upper elementary classrooms, appropriate use in the lower grades also allows the teacher to move from delivering information to the whole group, to supporting students individually and in small groups to support active construction of understandings. It also provides students with the opportunity for greater peer-mentoring when they can collaboratively access and make meaning of a direct lesson online, as many times as needed, before moving into the exploration phase of the learning.

Supporting Equitable Learning

Technology in the classroom can contribute to equitable learning for all students. Scaffolding for struggling readers through text to speech technology opens up a world of resources that were previously unavailable for learning. The reverse, speech to text technology, allows students whose writing skills may challenge them to put their thoughts on paper and creates a whole new realm of possibility for storytelling, journal writing, opinion sharing, and much more. Digital art and creation software facilitates the alignment of students' knowledge and thinking with the requirement of education policy for skills demonstration. Too often students have abilities, understandings, and ideas that go unnoticed because they are unable to write them down or articulate them in an oral presentation.

THROUGH THE WINDOW...

A young boy consciously did a half-hearted job on a speech he was required to write because he was fearful of being selected to perform it aloud. The result met his criterion as he was not selected, but his grade did not reflect his ability to craft an excellent speech.

What if he had had the opportunity to record, edit, review, and re-record his thoughts without standing in front of a classroom? Perhaps the speech would have been much stronger and the grade much higher. Technology in the classroom allows us to level the field so that each student has the opportunity to show teachers the true value of their thinking and learning.

Working with teacher candidates in the investigation of how each of us learns, students in our faculty had been asked to write a paper on an experience with learning something difficult. It was a strong exercise in metacognitive thinking (thinking about their thinking and learning) and the value of self-assessing their optimal learning styles. The assignment produced an interesting array of essays on everything from learning to ride a bicycle to learning how to cope with tragic life events. Nevertheless, it was clear that students who were adept at writing creatively had a far easier time with the task. If we were truly going to study how people learn, then the assignment needed to consider how students were permitted to present their learning.

When students were permitted to submit their work using any medium, results were astounding. Every year my office overflowed with paintings, art, audio-visual presentations, interpretive dance videos, sculptures, recorded speeches, songs, spoken word, children's books, and traditional essays. I was impressed by the depth of understanding and thinking that my students showed in their work, a richness that I had not seen as consistently in their essays the prior year. Many former teacher candidates spoke about using the strategy with their own students and how impactful it had been. Some indicated how they had modified it to work with younger children who created word art, collages, poems, podcasts, and dramatizations to represent their learning. All expressed how student success and engagement in learning increased when learners were able to represent their understandings through various types of technology, media, and art forms in addition to traditional ways.

ACTION STRATEGY: WHAT I KNOW

What...
What I Know is a strategy that asks students to consider how they can best present their learning and makes available a variety of ways to demonstrate their understanding. While some students may choose to demonstrate their learnings using written text, some may choose to use presentation technology (PowerPoint, Prezi, etc.), and others may choose to dramatize their understanding or provide a graphic design, visual narrative, podcast, or video presentation.

Implementation

How...

Teachers open the door for alternate modes of presentation when demonstrations of understanding, rather than modes of presentation, are being assessed. Students should be encouraged to experiment with differing modes of demonstrating their knowledge to expand their experience and exposure to new ways of sharing what they know, and to become adept in the use of new skills and technologies.

Why...

To be equitable for all students, the demonstration of their learning or understandings should not be limited to writing a journal, essay, story, or other text-based format. While strong writers will excel, students who are challenged to create written text will be disadvantaged if required to use a written format. Certainly students who struggle with writing need support to develop their skills; however, assessment of their subject knowledge in science, mathematics, or social studies will be far more accurate when students are given the opportunity to use alternate modes and media to demonstrate their learning.

What If...

What if we thought about demonstrations of learning in other subject areas in much the same way we think of assessment in physical education classes? Assessment in gym class is not based on the students' ability to write about basketball. Following that train of thought, why would we assess students' understanding of plants, electricity, history, or geography based on written text? Even within language class, students' understanding of the elements of a story might be just as accurately demonstrated by creating a storyboard as it would be by writing a paragraph to explain their understanding.

A primary student may struggle to write a story. Understanding of the format or elements of a story may not be evident in the student's written product. However, if asked to create a digital (or hard copy) storyboard, the student may be able to demonstrate a clear understanding of setting, characters, beginning, middle, and end, along with problem and resolution. Perhaps if the student were asked to retell the story from the storyboard, the oral process would provide even further insights into such learning as character development or the use of descriptive language.

Imagine the difference in a report card evaluation for struggling primary writers when the opportunity for alternate modes of demonstrating learning are employed. Using only the written product, an evaluation might read, "Student A demonstrates a limited awareness of the elements of a story." Using an alternate mode to demonstrate learning, such as a storyboard, the report card might read, "Using a storyboard, Student A demonstrates a good understanding of the elements of a story. Student A is able to retell the story and is working towards putting it down in writing." In an equitable and inclusive classroom community, every student has equal opportunity to demonstrate their learning.

Collaborating through Technology

Having recently gone through a period where technology seemed to consume schooling due to a global pandemic that forced many schools to move to synchronous or asynchronous virtual learning, many of us have found that the sense of community in our classrooms has been challenged. Students in the younger grades struggle to focus in an online environment, students in the upper elementary grades struggle to engage, often replacing their camera feed with an onscreen photo or graphic image.

In conversations with teachers, it appears there is no easy answer, but balance seems to be a key factor that helped some classroom communities remain intact and develop in cases where the school year required full-time online learning. Balance between synchronous and asynchronous learning, and between whole groups and breakout groups when synchronous learning was in place, allowed students to pace their learning. However, many students intimated that the lack of socialization in the online learning experience left them feeling isolated.

Collaboration is central to creating and maintaining a community. Collaborative thinking initiated through patterned writing is an ideal way to help students connect, learn to collaborate more effectively, and gain insights into other perspectives that spur deeper thinking. It often begins by using a read-aloud book to provide the pattern. Students then collaborate and negotiate to create their group's pattern.

An example that works successfully for students of all ages is based on the format of *The Important Book* (Wise Brown, 1949). The author names a succession of objects and selects the "important thing" about each object (spoon, apple, snow, etc.). The pattern in the book begins with "The important thing about _____ is…." The pattern continues with four or five lines that provide alternative responses, and then ends with a repeat of the first line. The subject or topic is limitless, as are the responses that students can create. The challenge is that the final product must reflect only four or five key points, the initial most important point followed by three or four others, and finally a repetition of the initial statement "The most important thing about _____ is…."

In small breakout groups or in person, students collaborate to write their pattern. This usually requires much discussion, negotiation, and consensus building as there are clearly many important things about any topic, but the group must choose only one as the key statement and limit supplementary statements.

ACTION STRATEGY: PATTERNED WRITING

What…

Patterned Writing is a strategy that uses a simple picture book format and patterned writing to stimulate thinking, create consensus, and support student collaboration. Students can use the format of a published book as a template that is independent from the original text or can visualize their work as adding a page to the existing text.

Group work can be shared with the whole class in various formats to note common themes, unique ideas, and strategies used for creating, negotiating, and coming to consensus on the content of the group's patterned writing.

Implementation

How…

The teacher selects a book that uses a pattern of writing to express ideas. The book pattern then becomes a template for students to follow. The template can be applied to any number of curriculum areas to initiate student thinking. Students brainstorm ideas of how they will complete the template, collaborate to come to consensus on what the final product will look like, and prepare a "page" that will be displayed in digital form (PowerPoint, Prezi, etc.) or in print form on chart paper for a gallery walk. Examples of texts that lend themselves well to this process are:

- *The Important Book* (Brown, 1949) Consider curricular themes — "The important thing about science is…" — or learning themes — "The important thing about curiosity is…"
- "The House that Jack Built" (Traditional Rhyme) Consider environmental themes — "This is the plastic bottle that…"
- *May We Have Enough to Share* (VanCamp, 2019) Consider creating ideals for the classroom community — "May we have empathy when we listen to each other."
- *If You Give a Moose a Muffin* (Numeroff, 1991) Consider potential for learning or good works — "If you give a kid a pencil…" or "If you give a friend a hand…"

If you don't have these books in your school library, check out YouTube read-alouds.

Why…

Simple patterned writing is a great way to stimulate thought and encourage even reluctant writers. Working on the pattern as a group using a common theme supports the development of collaborative learning and consensus building skills and provides a variety of perspectives.

What If…

The "what if" potential for patterned writing is limitless. This strategy used in primary classrooms, university lecture halls, or professional development sessions always yields great ideas and much wisdom, along with a shared or renewed sense of purpose and collaboration. *The House that Crack Built* (Taylor, 1992) uses patterned writing to address drug abuse and can support in-school drug awareness programs.

An example of student work using community as a theme might result in a group creating a pattern based on the *Important Book* (Brown, 1949).

The important thing about community is that I belong.
It is a safe place to be.
It helps me to grow.
It builds friendships.
But the important thing about community is that I belong.

Once the text has been created, it can be embedded in a class presentation through a shared document, visual presentation set to music, or writing on paper that can be posted on the classroom walls to allow students to complete a gallery walk to view the work of other groups. To wrap up, students go back to their groups and discuss what surprised them, confirmed their understanding, or made them think differently after seeing the work of other groups. They also reflect upon and articulate the strategies they used to create, negotiate, and come to consensus on the final product.

This activity works well with any topic. The important thing about plants is… The important thing about *Little House on the Prairie* (Wilder, 1935) is… The important thing about math is… The list is endless.

Assessment outside the Box

When students are working together to mentor each other in learning, collaborating in developing new ideas, and demonstrating their learning in a variety of modes including oral communication, the conversation about accurate assessment is always front and centre. Talk takes place in the moment. It is a reality that disappears unless recorded.

THROUGH THE WINDOW...

Beyond the lost physical indicators, recorded conversations require hours of playback…hours that I do not have outside the classroom day. When I think of recorded interactions with students, I am reminded of the time I decided to videotape my daughter's dance recital. It was a disaster. I was seated quite far from the stage. Consequently, I ended up with a low quality recording of the heads of people in front me and my daughter in the background. I did not realize until I watched the playback that I had missed the excitement of her performance by only seeing it through the screen on my device. I was not present in the moment and I had failed to capture the essence of the performance. It was all disappointing.

For busy teachers, it can be truly frightening to think that a moment that provides evidence of learning might be missed and unavailable to inform report cards and parent interviews. Written work can be saved in a notebook or on a test paper or in a worksheet. Talk is fleeting.

I have attempted recording oral interactions with students or between students in breakout groups. Sadly, it never seems to meet my needs. Listening to the recordings does not allow me to be present in the moment. While a device may be recording student conversations, it does not capture the nuances that make classroom talk rich and informative. The facial expressions, the body language, and the personal mannerisms that are all an integral part of the message are lost in a recording.

From the beginning I loved the implementation of a collaborative, talk-rich classroom community where students worked together and mentored each other in their learning, but I despaired over how I might gather the high level of assessment information that was needed to effectively evaluate students' progress against mandated curricular outcomes.

So I asked this question:

How might methods of assessment of student learning transform to reflect the realities of a talk-rich, collaborative community?

Assessment, like everything else in education, needs to exist in a state of balance. A single form of assessment will not accurately reflect a student's understanding. Nevertheless, in many classrooms written assessment is the norm. It is easy to manage and provides hard evidence to support reporting to parents and school districts. The downside of traditional written assessments or text is that even though students may be writing at or approaching grade level, the understandings, explorations, wonderings, and enthusiasms that teachers witness during learning conversations are often not evident in the writing tasks used for assessment. In addition, struggling writers are greatly challenged by writing-based assessment tasks, even with the support of voice to text technology. On the other hand, assessment of collaborative learning and talk-based explorations using the same criteria as written assessment leaves a teacher madly scrambling to record performance without the ability to be fully present in the moment.

Working with the criterion that a teacher needs to be fully present with the student to generate accurate assessment, it is impossible to assess everyone at one time. However, it is possible to assess each student individually if there is a plan in place to oversee *all* but focus on *one*. Here's how it works:

On paper only, the teacher divides the class into five groups (A–E). The groups do not need to align with a seating plan, since the teacher is focusing on only one student at a time. Therefore, in a class of twenty-five students the teacher focuses on five students per day. Focusing on a student does not mean hovering over that student every minute. It simply means spending a little extra time with that student over the course of the day, making a few jot notes, observing where the student is relative to the optimal learning outcomes for the activity, and engaging in conversation with the student to assess their progress. Observing four, five, or even six focal students per day does not increase the teacher's workload but significantly increases opportunities to assess their learning.

Since every student is methodically observed and assessed every week, the teacher develops far greater insights into each student's understandings and learning needs over time, rather than on testing day or in one particular assignment. The daily assessments are cross-curricular over the course of the day. Given that every student is a focal student once per week, there is plenty of opportunity over the term to get a strong sense of each student's progress in all subjects.

At the end of the week, the teacher will have completed a focused observation and assessment of each student in the class. If a student is absent on their assessment day, it is not critical. Over the course of the term, weekly assessments provide teachers with strong evidence of learning.

The plan does not preclude the use of other assessment tools such as written work, projects, or presentations. However, the need to implement frequent tests decreases along with the amount of grading required. For those students whose developing oral skills require a prompt to support extended talk, teachers can encourage the use of visual representations of their understandings (graphics, charts, plans, or jot notes) to assist them as they develop their oral skills. This combination creates a more equitable and balanced assessment.

The assessment plan works on a five-day rotation that changes weekly so that one student, for example, does not become a *Monday* student. In the rotation below, the students in Group A are assessed on Monday. The following week, the students in Group A are assessed on Tuesday; the following week, the students in Group A are assessed on Wednesday, etc.

Week 1	Monday	Tuesday	Wednesday	Thursday	Friday
Group A	X				
Group B		X			
Group C			X		
Group D				X	
Group E					X
Week 2	Monday	Tuesday	Wednesday	Thursday	Friday
Group A		X			
Group B			X		
Group C				X	
Group D					X
Group E	X				
Week 3	Monday	Tuesday	Wednesday	Thursday	Friday
Group A			X		
Group B				X	
Group C					X
Group D	X				
Group E		X			

There is an ancillary benefit of getting to know students much better, which results in more open and interesting learning conversations. Through careful questioning in classroom conversations, the teacher is able to gain deeper insights into students' subject or process knowledge and their understandings of a concept or theory. The focused learning conversations encourage students to think critically and to examine their own metacognitive processes in the moment, rather than through written comments in the margin of a written piece of work. For planning purposes, ongoing insights into student learning ensure that planning meets the needs of all students.

Once the plan is in place, the system is easy to follow. The teacher continues to observe and monitor all students daily, while the focal students receive the teacher's particular attention. The rotation chart ensures each student receives the teacher's targeted attention for assessment purposes every week, but not always on the same day of the week.

Tip:
Ensure your assessment groups
are not the same as the students'
working groups. This facilitates your
movement around the classroom,
allowing you to monitor and/or
respond to all students throughout
the day.

Students continue to keep science journals, write stories, and undertake assignments or projects; however, those text-based assignments generally serve the teacher's need to assess student writing skills within a curriculum subject.

A favorite question for learning conversations with focal students is "How do you know?" It's a perfect way to confirm that surface understandings are based on accurate information. Students are encouraged to *wonder aloud* to facilitate digging deeper into the learning. Other prompts to facilitate talk-based assessment of student learning include:

- Tell me about your thinking as you worked your way through this (process, task, activity).
- What facts, understandings, or presumptions led you to that conclusion?
- Where do you think this learning will lead you?

Using classroom talk in assessment allows teachers to build stronger professional relationships with students. Realizing that their voices are valued in the classroom, students begin to gain greater confidence in themselves as learners. In articulating their understandings of curriculum, and of society, life, technology, and so much more, students take greater interest in their learning and that of their peers. Students listening to and participating in the teacher's learning conversations with the *focal student* witness a model of communication that they can emulate. Many an "aha" moment comes out of listening to students sharing their passions for and challenges with learning, their wonderings about the world, and their opinions on everything under (and beyond) the sun.

Finally, teachers who undertake talk-based assessment find that a rating scale is more user-friendly than letter or numerical grading. These levels generally correspond to grading systems across regions.

At the "what" level students are able to perceive what the teacher is modeling although they exhibit little understanding of the concept and are challenged to replicate it. At the "how" level, the students are able to independently reproduce the activity or the teacher-modeled task; however, there is only basic understanding of the concept that underlies the activity. At the "why" level, the students are able to recognize the activity, reproduce it independently, and relate to the concept with an understanding of why it works. At the "what if" level, the students are able to extend their understanding to apply and restructure the learning to fit alternative scenarios.

Similarly, simple levels of comprehension — "retell", "relate", and "reflect" — can support teachers to observe students meaning-making skills (Schwartz and Bone, 1995). At the "retell" level, students are able to recite or regurgitate learning. At the "relate" level, students are able to relate the learning to their own experience or to other sources (media, text, world view). Finally, at the "reflect" level, students are able to think critically about the learning. When observing students using the weekly assessment rotation, it is most helpful to use these straightforward criteria on a daily basis. Trying to assign a numeric or alpha grade during learning conversations with focal students is generally impractical.

These levels are simple for students to understand and use for self-assessment, too. Introduced to the concept, even young students will be able to consider a topic and learn to self-assess whether they understand what, how, why, or what if, encouraging metacognitive development and providing students with a concrete path for improvement. Assessment at any grade level must accurately reflect the student's level of learning, but also be transparent to a student who wants to improve their learning.

4

Leaders in Learning

I recall with some embarrassment, when I had to teach electricity to my grade 5 students. This being my first year in a grade 5 classroom, I was still refreshing my fact base and understandings and, to be quite honest, I did not know much about electricity. I had a generalized understanding of the process and recalled that if my holiday lights were wired in series then when one bulb went out the whole string was out... or was that parallel? I remembered the story of Benjamin Franklin with the key tied to a kite, and I knew that if my dishwasher refused to start, I could reset the breaker and it would reboot the control panel and I could wash my dishes. I also knew it was time for a new dishwasher.

Prior to my lesson, I called my father for a refresher course in electricity. He laughingly bemoaned the fact that he was still helping me with my homework, then set about to explain it all to me in some detail. Despite his tutoring, I still felt woefully unprepared to teach my lesson and was totally convinced that making a battery from a potato in the classroom would be an abject failure. I felt like a fraud going into a classroom to teach children something that I had not mastered. How could I evaluate their knowledge at the end of the electricity unit when I knew that I would barely merit a passing grade?

After wrestling between "Can I fake it until I make it?" and "Will this be a disaster?" I realized that I was asking myself the wrong questions. I should have been asking, "How might I make this unit a rich learning experience for my students?" When I asked that question, I immediately came up with an answer. Rather than attempting to pretend I was an expert in electricity, I would share with my students my true expertise: how to be a learner.

When it came time to begin our unit on electricity, I headed to school with my hairdryer. I plugged it in at the front of the classroom and proceeded to fluff my hair. Of course, the students laughed and then asked me what I was doing. I carefully explained that all I knew about electricity was that if I plugged an electrical appliance into a wall outlet, it worked thanks to electricity. How the electricity got to our classroom from Niagara Falls was still outside of my sphere of understanding.

It was interesting to see the range of student reactions. Some students were puzzled. How could the teacher not know everything? Others seemed a bit relieved. Well, if she doesn't know, it lets me off the hook. And some were quite excited. They were eager to teach me what they knew and eager to figure out together the pieces that we were collectively missing.

For our unit on electricity, I took on the role of lead learner. I mentored students by sharing my understandings of how I learn something new. They mentored me by sharing their prior knowledge and the new understandings they created as we collaborated to build our collective understandings. It was an extraordinary experience for all of us.

Clearly, I am not suggesting that teachers abdicate their responsibility to know the curriculum they are teaching. However, particularly in the elementary grades when teachers are delivering all subjects across the curriculum, it is reasonable to admit that we are all ongoing learners.

In my region, the Ontario College of Teachers' Standards of Practice (https://www.oct.ca) require that all teachers be ongoing learners. I wonder how often we actually demonstrate this to our students. How often in the busy-ness of a school day do we share with students the new things that interest us and propel our professional and personal learning? What if we modeled our enthusiasm for learning new skills, concepts, hobbies, and ways of thinking? What if we encouraged our students to do the same as part of their learning conversations so that they might discover who they are as learners, in what ways they best learn, and what triggers their desire to engage with new learning?

This experience encouraged me to continue thinking about the impact of co-mentoring between teacher and students, and between students and their peers. In my classroom, I had witnessed a real commitment to the learning when the students were engaged with supporting others, and me, with their learning. There was a greater confidence in seeking new understandings demonstrated by students who collaborated in their learning. There was a clear give and take as students alternated between leading the learning and being mentored by a peer. Finally, there was an overall sense of satisfaction and ownership of the learning after successfully completing the unit and developing shared understandings.

This experience also shifted my perspective on my role in the classroom. I realized that I did not always need to be the expert or even the lead learner in the classroom. My students had demonstrated to me that they had the capacity to take on leading and mentoring roles to varying degrees when given the opportunity. They also demonstrated a greater willingness to be mentored by a peer when they realized that it was not simply a one-way street, and that their understandings were of value to me and to classmates.

Seeing students assume the role of lead learner and mentor to their peers convinced me to open up curriculum investigations to broader learning. For example, students learning about electricity also ended up exploring the social implications of issues in our community. Students examined the pros and cons of wind power, solar energy, and the NIMBY (Not in My Backyard) movements that often brought local community pressure to bear on environmental decisions. They became interested in the impact of hydro-generating stations on local waterways, aquatic plants, and wildlife. Our collaborative investigation empowered students who sought to learn above and beyond the curriculum requirements, while also engaging the less enthusiastic learners through the impetus of the class commitment. While we learned about electricity as a form of energy, we learned much about the collective and potential energy of our classroom as a community, and how we might become mentors, partners, and leaders in learning for each other.

Thinking about Thinking

Remembering, or more accurately, the failure to remember is one of the first concerns that come to mind for adults when we are asked to reflect on cognitive abilities. We all have those moments when we find it difficult to remember the name of someone we meet in the street, or the reason we've gone downstairs. While healthy lifestyle habits, staying mentally active, and engaging in social activity all help to maintain memory function, I often wonder if it is this adult concern with having it or losing it that has made memory work such a traditional part of so many classrooms. Indeed, a good memory is helpful so that we can quickly use stored multiplication table calculations to figure out a tip in a restaurant, but much of what we work so hard to remember in school is no longer valuable information.

So I asked this question:

How might peer mentoring provide opportunities for students to consistently think at a higher level and thereby increase their capacity for learning beyond memorization?

THROUGH THE WINDOW...

A colleague was madly struggling with an uncooperative photocopier on a Friday at lunch. She was copying a test that she was planning to give that afternoon. Witnessing her frustration, I suggested she wait and give the test on Monday. She looked at me and said, "Are you kidding? These kids won't remember this stuff by Monday." Of course, we both laughed at the absurdity of the situation. However, the reality of the teacher's comment has stayed with me and greatly impacted my practice.

Stepping away from the stance of expecting students, regardless of grade level, to *know or remember facts* moves teachers towards the expectation that students *think and learn* using mental processes to apply their understandings to further explorations. In asking students to know, it is simply a matter of repetition and reinforcement until students memorize it. If you still remember when Columbus sailed, you probably memorized this line from an old poem,

In 1492 Columbus sailed the ocean blue.

While memory can be useful in many situations, it is not nearly enough. This is particularly true when you can open your phone and ask when Columbus sailed if you are in immediate need of that information. When memorization is used as an exercise for mental agility, it can be a useful tool. It is less useful as a tool for cognitive development.

In asking students to *think*, teachers need to provide tools that work across the curriculum and are best suited to the learning needs of individual students. When students are introduced to a manner of thinking about learning and have the opportunity to practice it, they will begin to use it independently as they think about and discuss their learning.

The following is an example from a grade 2 classroom where the students were asked to demonstrate their thinking while solving a two-digit math problem.

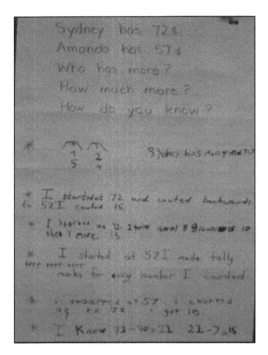

THROUGH THE WINDOW...

Sydney has 72 cents. Amanda has 57 cents. Who has more? How much more? How do you know?

Thinking about "how" they knew the answer, students working in groups recorded their processes on a chart. The chart recorded the insight into students' thinking and facilitated a great discussion on which method was the most efficient. It also forced students to move beyond simply coming up with the answer without understanding *why* 72-57=15, or that the difference between 72 and 57 is also 15. The lesson ended with students discovering that subtraction was only one way of determining the difference between two numbers.

Student #1 created a place value chart to determine Sydney has more groups of 10 and, therefore, more money. Student #1 knew who had more by simply looking at the 10s column. This provided the teacher with the insight that the student understood place value, at least to the 10s. However, the student did not bother to precisely calculate how much more.

10s	1s
7	2
5	7

Student #2, realizing that this was a subtraction problem, started at 72 and counted backwards to figure out how many to take away to reach 57, eventually coming up with 15.

Student #3 started at 57 and counted up using tally marks. This was an eye-opener for a number of the students who previously thought of subtraction as a "take away" rather than the difference between two numbers.

Student #4 started at 57 and counted up to 72 but used counters rather than tally marks.

Student #5 demonstrated to classmates that 57 is actually 50 plus 7 more, so did the easy mental math calculation of 72-50 to get 22, then subtracted 7 to get 15.

Having a window into the thinking of their peers facilitated new ways of manipulating numbers to find difference and resulted in a much clearer understanding of subtraction and place value. After discussion, the students generally agreed that making tally marks and counting backwards was not the most efficient way to the solve the problem, even though it resulted in the correct answer. Most started to experiment with breaking down numbers to do mental math, as modeled by Student #5. This example of peer mentoring allowed many students to move from the "what", "how", and "why" of the problem to the "what if" level. After all, what is the subtraction by regrouping method other than a short cut, which, if not fully unpacked, leaves students stuck at the "how" level?

Discussing their solutions, students created new understandings of why it was important to be able to solve problems like this. Some considered that if they only had 72 cents and wanted to buy something for 57 cents, they could figure it out first, then decide if it was worth making the purchase knowing they would only have 15 cents left. This initial concept in financial literacy led to thinking about budgeting money and making wise purchasing decisions.

Traditionally, this lesson might have been taught using standard methodology for subtraction. All students could have memorized the procedure of starting with the ones column, "borrowing" a group of "ten 1s" from the tens column to subtract 7 from 12, then subtracting 5 from the 6 remaining groups of 10 in the tens column. However, this thinking often confuses students who simply regroup by rote with little understanding of place value. The collaborative and talk-rich method of solving in a variety of ways provided deeper understandings, including:

- Subtraction is about finding the difference between two numbers.
- 72 is not simply 7 and 2. It is 7 groups of 10 and 2 more.
- Numbers can be broken down and regrouped for easier mental math calculations.
- Some methods of calculation are more efficient than others, even though the answer is the same.
- Real world implications about money and budgeting are relevant to students' lives.

This activity also provides students with insight into what works for them as individual learners. One student might realize that the tally marks are cumbersome but perhaps beneficial at this point in the learning. This understanding might also help the student to set goals and seek alternate strategies, such as breaking down numbers into *friendlier* chunks that make problem solving easier. While students will differ in how they learn and in the key strategies that are most effective for their learning, the awareness of these key strategies and their implementation in a learning environment facilitates their ongoing learning. Providing students with the opportunity to experiment with strategies for learning and observe the strategies used by the teacher and their peers provides them with a foundational understanding upon which they can launch their own inquiries into ongoing learning.

Another key strategy is considering alternative ways of knowing. Each of us sees the world through a lens of our experience. Asking students to attempt to look through an alternative lens opens up their thinking to new perspectives. For example, teaching children how to count to 10 and beyond in Mandarin will provide a unique lens in learning place value. Numbers beyond ten are represented by their place value (21 = two ten one).

```
1)  一  Yī
2)  二  Èr
3)  三  Sān
4)  四  Sì
5)  五  Wǔ
6)  六  Liù
7)  七  Qī
8)  八  Bā
9)  九  Jiǔ
10) 十  Shí
```

Imagine how easily students will visualize 21, or any other number, and how much fun children will have impressing their families with their ability to count to 100 in Mandarin and internalize understandings of place value at the same time.

There are a number of online websites and YouTube videos where you can hear the pronunciation of the numbers and see how each number is constructed. It is a valuable way to learn for teacher and students.

To help students understand the importance of looking at more than one way of knowing, teachers can respectfully acknowledge and share the process referred to as "Two-Eyed Seeing" (Marshall, 2004).

ACTION STRATEGY: WAYS OF KNOWING

What…

Sharing a practice that supports the recognition of differing perspectives, Mi'kmaq Elder Albert Marshall (Bartlett, Marshall, and Marshall, 2015) states, "Two-Eyed Seeing refers to learning to see from one eye with the strengths of Indigenous ways of knowing and from the other eye with the strengths of Western ways of knowing and to using both of these eyes together". Across the curriculum in science, history, language, arts, mathematics, and literature, exposing students to alternative ways of knowing prepares them to engage with a global community that includes many ways of knowing.

Implementation

How...

A simple way to encourage students to look at alternative perspectives is to ask them to study a topic from another's point of view. How would decisions to open agricultural space to housing development impact a farmer living in the area? How would it impact someone who does not have access to affordable housing? How would it impact food security in the greater community? What would local wildlife tell us if they could talk? To introduce this concept through picture books, consider reading *The Great Kapok Tree: A Tale of the Amazon Rain Forest* (Cherry, 2000) with your students. Ask your students to dramatize the story with each taking on the role of a different animal and adding dialogue to the author's text. Young students might consider what a polar bear thinks about climate change, or a whale thinks about plastic water bottles.

Why...

Albert Marshall defines *Etuaptmumk* — Two-Eyed Seeing — as "the gift of multiple perspective treasured by many Aboriginal peoples". The Institute for Integrative Science and Health in Nova Scotia states, "We believe it is the requisite Guiding Principle for the new consciousness needed to enable Integrative Science work, as well as other integrative or transcultural or transdisciplinary or collaborative work." http://www.integrativescience.ca/Principles/TwoEyedSeeing/

What If...

What if considering alternate perspectives was every student's "go to" strategy for any inquiry or study in the classroom? Imagine how much richer the learning would be.

An important protocol in sharing Elder Albert Marshall's work with students is the acknowledgment of the source. When we help students to recognize and appreciate the source of alternative ways of knowing, we strengthen their determination to consider alternative perspectives and to acknowledge that there are many lenses through which people can see the world.

If we help students to become open-minded and collaborative in considering new ideas, concepts, and ways of thinking and being in the world, they will become adults who can overcome obstacles and solve problems in empathetic and innovative ways.

Students who fail to see beyond what they know, or think they know, risk becoming so mired in the swamp of their own way of looking at the world that they don't see when someone is throwing them a lifeline. In a classroom community where students appreciate alternative perspectives, there are always others who can mentor them through a problem and provide differing views of the world.

To implement the process of examining more than one perspective for younger students, it is interesting to ask them to choose an animal, object, statue, building, or historical personage and centre their inquiry around what their chosen focus may have observed or witnessed. Studying weather or climate patterns, what might be the polar bear's perspective? How would the polar bear's perspective differ from the perspective of the Amazon milk frog? For inquiry into the historical events of World War II, what might be the perspective of the Eiffel Tower? What might Ben Franklin have to say about the use of electricity in the 21st century, or Alexander Graham Bell about cellular phones? The questions for inquiry and the lenses presented are limited only by the creativity of students. How might teachers enhance the curriculum by providing opportunities to fully engage with and explore a topic, issue, or event through a lens that differs from the student's experience?

In the past, the availability of resource texts in a school library may have impacted a student's ability to inquire deeply into a focal aspect of a particular curriculum topic. However, with the availability of online resources today, it is quite easy to allow students to tailor their curriculum-mandated learning to their interests. And while previously it might have been common for all students to create a similar culminating project, it is a far richer experience for each student to undertake an inquiry that is relevant to them and to broaden the classroom community's understandings by sharing their work with peers. "Having a joint interest, a common interest, so that one is eager to give and the other to take" (Dewey, 1916) is foundational to creating deeper thinking. Dewey continues, "It contrasts with telling or stating things simply for the sake of impressing them upon another".

An interesting way to encourage a student to consider alternative perspectives is to ask them to learn about a current major event and write about it in a letter to their future grandchild. What would they say? What would they choose to include, what would they leave out? How would their perspective change in writing to a child of their future? What implications for the future might the writer speculate about as a result of the event? If you were to write to a future grandchild about the global pandemic of 2020/2021, what would you say? It is a thought-provoking exercise.

Too often students see themselves solely in relation to their past experience. Students who have not been great at math in prior years will presume that math is "just not their subject". However, a change of lens or perspective can also lead to a change of attitude and result in greater student success. A look into how a student has learned or failed to learn in the past can help them to develop new ways of learning that will yield greater success in the future. Linking to the "what", "how", "why", "what if" assessment tool (see p. 72), teachers can support students by consistently asking, "How do you know?" Once the student gets into the habit of answering that question, they will begin to ask it of themselves and recognize the patterns that yield successful learning. However, before students come to that point of recognition, it is often helpful to see themselves as successful in an aspect of curriculum that will lead to future success.

ACTION STRATEGY: MATHEMAGICIANS

What...

Mathemagicians is a strategy that reminds students to look beyond the answer and understand the "how and why" of a process through pattern recognition. It provides an example of how student participation in an activity can create classroom community and confidence in learning by allowing students to consider simple math problems and unpack "how" they know the answer and "why" it works. A grade 2 class used this strategy to "dazzle" their parents at the school open house and sparked many home and school conversations about math and learning.

Implementation

How...

Students are given a simple math problem to solve that begins with someone thinking of a number and writing it on a piece of paper. The Mathemagician, a student in the classroom, then asks another student, person or visitor, to do a few simple calculations to come up with a new number. For example, add 5, take away 2, add 7, take away 8. The calculation results in a net gain of 2. The Mathemagician asks the student to reveal their "new number", then with an abracadabra is able to identify the original number which, in this example, will be 2 less than the "new number". This calculation works for grade 2; more complex calculations can be devised for higher grades.

Why...

While this may seem like magic for students, it is a lesson in calculation. It can be used to facilitate learning the rules for ordering (BEDMAS = brackets, exponents, division, multiplication, addition, and subtraction) and developing thinking skills through mental math. However, the true magic lies beyond the mathematical learning as this strategy helps students to build pattern recognition skills. The ability to seek and see patterns supports learning, decision making, predicting, logical reasoning, and making connections. It is also the foundation for computer coding and programming.

What If...

What if we provide students with opportunities to understand and explore how their expanding pattern recognition skills across the curriculum can open new avenues for inquiry and innovation? Art, music, and poetry are also excellent examples of patterning as a creative force. A simple strategy that begins as a game to dazzle family and friends can lead to skills development that opens up an exciting future when it is explicitly identified and explored in the classroom.

Each time a student has the opportunity to think about their thinking, understand the background to their perspective, and contrast it to the perspective of another, that student grows in their cognitive development. Each time a student steps outside themselves to think about how they learn and applies it strategically to future learning, that student becomes a metacognitive learner. And each time a student has the opportunity to lead their own learning through creative inquiry, they become a richer and more innovative thinker.

An Engaged Learning Community

The first thing teacher candidates or new teachers ask as they head to a first practicum placement or teaching position is how to *manage* a classroom. Much to their disappointment, there is no *Classroom Management Manual* with an A–Z foolproof method for managing students. When asked to provide my tips on classroom management, I generally advise that engaged students manage themselves quite well and professional relationship building with students is at the top of my priorities list for the school year.

I have to admit that the term classroom management does not sit well with me. In my mind the term evokes a top-down structure that presumes teacher control over all aspects of the classroom, including student behavior, which is based on rules, authority, power, and control. For me that description is the antithesis of community. Classroom management is not a protocol that one implements at the beginning of every year, rather it is a perception that results from an engaged learning community whose relationships, responsibilities, and routines are an integral part of the dynamic.

Having determined my understanding, I needed a way to articulate my philosophy to students in my teacher education classes.

So I asked this question:

Which affective factors underpin the creation of an engaged learning community?

Considering this question required a review of the characteristics of a learning day that went well and the characteristics of a challenging day in the classroom. When I took note of specific situations that positively impacted learning, they fell into three categories: relationship, responsibility, and routines. When those three pieces were in place, the class seemed to engage more readily and learning flowed more easily.

Relationship ✓

As I have noted in previous chapters, building strong professional relationships in the classroom is always my priority from the first minute that students walk into the classroom. The objective is not to control the classroom, rather it is to create an environment where students learn to self-regulate, collaborate, and build respectful relationships that result in a caring learning community.

Beyond the deeper psychology of how and what a child learns, children acquire knowledge from books, the internet, and other resources, but they learn the world from what they experience in it.

When students hear teachers using their names and the names of their classmates, they learn to call each person by their name, too. They know that pointing and shouting "Hey!" or referring to someone as "that kid" is not respectful and therefore not acceptable in the caring classroom community. When they experience a teacher attentively listening to what they have to say or asking them to talk about it further when time permits (and making sure it happens), they understand the importance of valuing everyone's voice in the classroom.

Expectations for students and teachers need to be high within the classroom, but it is also important to know that everyone makes mistakes. When teachers make a mistake, apologies should be swift and sincere so that students understand that it is important to take responsibility for mistakes and also to forgive.

A student couldn't find his lunch. Of course, the teacher went through the full set of questions: Is it under your coat on the coat hook? No! Is it in your backpack? No! Did you leave it in the hall when you took off your boots? No! The child was convinced someone had taken the lunch and began to ask everyone in a somewhat accusatory tone if they had taken it. The teacher offered to help look again and sure enough in the bottom of the backpack was a brown-bagged lunch to which the child responded, "But my mom always puts it in my lunch box."

The child began eating the lunch, then stopped and approached the teacher to ask to speak to the class. In a loud clear voice, that young child apologized for thinking someone had taken the lunch, then went to every student who had been directly questioned to offer an apology. To the credit of the other children, everyone accepted the apology graciously and went on eating their own lunch.

It was quite a remarkable moment in that community to see the value of a respectful classroom dynamic come to life. Clearly, this was not all about the dynamic in the classroom. No doubt, the child also had a home environment that was respectful of everyone in the family. However, this interaction highlighted the importance of students' actions and reactions in building relationships and creating a community experience in the classroom.

Responsibility ✓

When children in grades 3 and 4 were asked about the responsibilities they have in their classrooms, they immediately thought of chores such as stacking chairs at the end of the day and picking up lost pencils. When specifically asked about responsibility for learning, the children indicated that the teacher made "plans" and that they had no responsibility. In their minds, the word responsibility did not link with learning, and they did not see themselves having any responsibility for learning in the classroom. As one student indicated, "We do what the teacher tells us to do" (M., age nine, 2022). A parent of one of these students recalled visiting an alternative school with their child and observing how the students at the school initiated learning and opened inquiries based on curiosity. At first, her child had seemed a bit unsure of how to engage with the learning without teacher leadership, but soon followed the other children's lead and was happily immersed in his own explorations.

As a parent and as a teacher I have always believed in ensuring that everyone in the family, and in the classroom community, takes responsibility for contributing to the well-being of the whole, but my conversation with these grade 3 and 4 students set me to thinking about how we might make explicit to students that responsibility goes far beyond physical chores in the classroom.

Sharing responsibilities in a classroom, as in a family, lessens the burden on everyone. When the class is engaged in independent activity, students can collaborate quietly, not because it is a rule but because it is a responsibility that everyone shares to support a peaceful environment. A tool to help students manage their responsibility is a classroom noise meter.

ACTION STRATEGY: NOISE METER

What...

A noise meter is simply a visual cue to remind students to lower their voices when group conversations begin to infringe on each other, making listening and learning a challenge.

A scale placed in a visible spot in the classroom allows students to mark their perception of the noise level without interrupting group work. Each group assigns a monitor to keep an eye on the scale. When any student or the teacher moves the arrow to indicate the noise level is "high" or above, each group's monitor reminds their group to lower their voices.

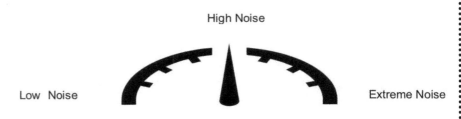

High Noise

Low Noise

Extreme Noise

Implementation

How...

The class agrees that low to moderate levels of conversation allow everyone to participate in group conversations. Group members take turns serving as a monitor who keeps an eye on the noise meter. If the teacher or any group feels that the noise level is impacting their ability to work effectively, the teacher or the group's monitor will move the arrow to indicate the need to lower voices. An audible signal such as a chime or bell can be used when the noise meter edges into the high zone. The teacher then speaks to the class using a soft voice to calm students. When noise levels are high, calling loudly for attention is ineffective and reinforces the acceptance of loud voices in the classroom. Using a soft voice requires students to quieten to hear the teacher. Similarly, if an individual student is shouting or becoming overwhelmed, a soft voice and tone from the teacher will help the student to reset to the teacher's model.

Why...

There are many times when a quiet classroom is best suited to an activity. When students are communicating and collaborating to learn, the sound of eager conversation is inevitable. However, conversation does not mean noise that disrupts group work and/or prevents students from hearing their group's conversation. Involving students in taking responsibility for monitoring noise levels and respecting everyone's need to hear what is happening in their group creates a learning environment that supports communication, collaboration, and community.

What If...

What if we took time to practice responding to the noise meter in the same way we practice responding to a fire drill? Students would soon learn the protocols to self-monitor noise levels.

Responsibility in the classroom is not limited to behaviors. Students are also responsible for their individual learning, for knowing when they need a break to breathe, for knowing when to ask for assistance, and for knowing when to offer assistance or mentor a peer. Students are also responsible for the collective work of the classroom.

Building collective responsibility means students often engage in group projects, or whole class undertakings such as publishing, fundraising, and event preparation. These types of activities build trust and relationships as students realize the personal satisfaction of achieving a shared objective and working together to get the job done. Such projects yield many opportunities for student mentoring. They also allow students to engage their specific talents and interests in the collective work. The student who struggles in one curriculum area can build confidence and self-esteem through demonstrating their artistic talents, research abilities, dramatic flair, or aptitude in other curriculum areas. Sharing responsibility for a project also helps students to understand that, in the real world, leadership is not the purview of one single person. A student who is a leader in an area of study or expertise benefits from the leadership of others in different areas of study or expertise as a project progresses. In sports, we encourage our students to function well as a team. Not everyone plays the same position and each brings different talents to the game. This philosophy works well in the classroom, too.

As teachers we need to ensure that each student has the opportunity to explore and learn so that they have a wide and bright future ahead of them. Giving them the opportunity to work collaboratively with others, and to mentor each as they reach a common goal, achieves two outcomes. Firstly, it allows students to "try on" different learning styles that others employ, explore different areas of learning through the eyes of other learners, and develop an understanding that what they have to contribute is of value. Secondly, and just as importantly, it creates a sense of responsibility to the community and to the learning outcomes. Responsibility in the classroom is not simply about stacking chairs.

Routines ✓

I often hear new and experienced teachers talking about classroom rules. In a collaborative learning community rules are few and created by the community for the common good. Generally, rules are based on the underlying values of the community. For example, rules might be as simple as:

- Speak with respect.
- Listen with attention.
- Care about others.

These simple rules handle just about any situation that arises. Routines should be established in a manner that responds to the needs of the students, the teacher, and the learning. When routines are in place organization happens naturally and the flow of the classroom is enhanced. The best thing about routines is that everybody knows the plan. For many students, the classroom can be a very stressful place. When there are routines in place, stress levels decrease for everyone and time lost to off-task behaviors and interactions is reduced.

The daily routines set expectations for students, provide structure and predictability to the day, and reinforce the spirit of community. When things go wrong and problems arise, students know that their voices will be heard. Routines that connect students to their goals and to each other enhance learning.

When unexpected frustrations erupt or energies collide, impromptu gatherings to "bring it back" support the community in regaining focus and resolving issues.

ACTION STRATEGY: BRINGING IT BACK

What…

Bringing It Back is a series of routines to support learning that set the tone for a harmonious classroom community. Students gather in a circle to share a daily intention or a personal concern or to address a community issue that needs resolution.

This strategy brings the class together in a manner that supports the well-being of all students by stopping, focusing on an action or intention, and finding their centre before moving on with their day.

Implementation

How…

Using the Action Strategy: Central Focus Design (see p. 54), which opens physical space for students to gather in a circle, these routines set the tone and reset the atmosphere throughout the day. Students gather twice each day to connect as a community. At other times, impromptu gatherings can bring students together to address an issue or discuss a common problem with the learning.

Beginning of the Day: Starting the day as a community establishes a feeling of connectedness that remains throughout the day. Young children gather in a circle on the carpet. Older students bring chairs and sit around the centre table. Students and teacher share with the group what their intention or objective is for the day. Once this routine is established there is always someone keen to speak first. This is also an opportunity for students to share with the community if there is something happening in their lives that the class needs to know to offer support or empathy. Students may offer an intention re: learning (To catch up with my science journal), behaviors (To stay on task with my math), or feelings (To stop and ask for help before I get frustrated). Personal concerns (A family member who was ill, or a pet who died) are listened to with empathy and care. When students seem adrift in the day, the teacher can ask, "Do you need to reset your intention for today?" For the student who shares a personal concern, it helps everyone to understand that a show of care and kindness may be needed to get through the day.

After Lunch Recess: After lunch recess, students immediately begin to read independently or take fifteen to twenty minutes to wind down. Many return to the classroom ready for some quiet time, while others are pumped up after a busy recess and require time to calm themselves so they can effectively attend to their learning. Soft classical or spa-type music reminds students to respect the quiet space. On occasion some students may choose to put their heads down and refresh. Others choose to read a book of their choice. Some catch up on unfinished work from the morning. Nobody moves around the classroom. When the students are able to attend to what they *need* in a peaceful and quiet environment, the rest of the afternoon flows more easily. At the end of the quiet time, students are ready to be on-task and productive. Establishing this routine supports the understanding that all students are responsible for their learning needs.

End of the Day: Students gather again in their circle. This is the time when questions and wonderings about the day's learning are raised, and where community problems are discussed and resolved. This is the time to share an interesting fact learned or a few words of wisdom gained during the day. Successes are shared and challenges are discussed. Students and teacher leave the classroom with a sense of closure to the day, appreciation for the learning, and readiness for the following day.

Why...
Explicitly connecting students to their goals and to each other enhances learning and creates community. When unexpected frustrations erupt or energies collide, impromptu gatherings to "bring it back" support the community in regaining focus and resolving issues.

What If...
What if the focus shifted from the lessons to the learner? Intrinsic motivation leads learning when the priority is establishing a frame of mind and sense of being that facilitates learning, collaboration, and community.

Students who are disengaged are generally uninterested, lacking challenge, bored, and/or feeling excluded from or unsuccessful in the learning. These students may disrupt others, act out, or zone out to totally detach themselves from the community. However, when the practices of offering support and differentiating instruction to meet the needs of all students becomes a daily routine, engagement increases.

Differentiating provides multiple access points for student learning. Teachers unfamiliar with differentiated instruction often fear that it means creating a separate lesson plan for every student in the classroom. They also worry that it will bog them down in assessment and evaluation. In reality, differentiated instruction does just the opposite. It allows students both voice and choice in their learning, which increases students' engagement by allowing them to apply learning strategies that they know work for them. It frees teachers to spend time in conversation with learners throughout the learning process and reduces the need to evaluate stacks of written work.

Differentiating instruction means that students have the opportunity to follow a variety of pathways to reach the learning objective. Some students may be accessing information independently online, some through text or video clips, while others may be sharing understandings through mentoring conversations with each other, or the teacher. Students will demonstrate their learning through a product that shares what they learned and, importantly, the questions they still have. Through conversation with students as they work through the learning and review of the culminating product (a journal for one student, a podcast for another, a video presentation or a poster board for others), the teacher is able to evaluate a student's depth and level of understanding (see Action Strategy: What I Know, p. 65).

Teachers who begin with an understanding that student engagement spurs success soon learn what interests their students. While not every student will be fully engaged in every curriculum topic, differentiated learning across the curriculum can support students in enhancing their fundamental skills in reading, writing, oral communication, inquiry, questioning, technology, and numeracy through contexts that are related to student interests. For example, a grade 3 class in our district studying "Communities in Canada: 1780-1850" in the social studies curriculum might inquire into then and now on a multitude of topics that relate to a variety of student interests including communication, commerce, environment, food, immigration, transportation, housing, clothing, literature, sports, health and wellness, or government. Gallery presentations turn everyone's interest and expertise into an enhanced learning experience for all.

Teachers can reach out to school support networks and to each other to implement the differentiation process in the classroom. Special education resource teachers can provide support with strategies to accommodate students who may need assistive technology, extra support to build literacy skills, or strategies for self-regulation.

How is there time to do this each day? Amazingly, the time makes itself available when the routines are in place. The classroom becomes a calmer and more productive place when relationships, responsibilities, and routines are understood by the community. Negative interactions between students that charge the air are less frequent. When students feel that they are valued in the community and their voices are heard, in turn they value the community and the shared learning. Instructional time runs more smoothly and less time is wasted during the day.

Living Curriculum

At various points in my career in education I have had the opportunity to work in collaboration with our local government in support of new teachers and new curriculum. In doing so I learned something that I wish someone had told me all those years ago when I began teaching. Curriculum is a statement of what students should know at the end of a grade or unit. It generally provides suggested routes to achieve the overall outcomes. However, these suggested routes are provided to support teachers and not to become a long list of boxes that must be ticked or activities that must be undertaken. The curriculum is a living document that recognizes the diverse needs of students. Therefore, curriculum is open to a variety of implementations that allow students to see themselves reflected in the learning and are meaningful to students' realties.

In our area, the wording of the curriculum expectations for reading in grades 1 and in grade 7 is identical:

GRADE 1 | READING

OVERALL EXPECTATIONS

By the end of Grade 1, students will:

1. read and demonstrate an understanding of a variety of literary, graphic, and informational texts, using a range of strategies to construct meaning;

2. recognize a variety of text forms, text features, and stylistic elements and demonstrate understanding of how they help communicate meaning;

3. use knowledge of words and cueing systems to read fluently;

4. reflect on and identify their strengths as readers, areas for improvement, and the strategies they found most helpful before, during, and after reading.

GRADE 1

GRADE 7 | READING

OVERALL EXPECTATIONS

By the end of Grade 7, students will:

1. read and demonstrate an understanding of a variety of literary, graphic, and informational texts, using a range of strategies to construct meaning;

2. recognize a variety of text forms, text features, and stylistic elements and demonstrate understanding of how they help communicate meaning;

3. use knowledge of words and cueing systems to read fluently;

4. reflect on and identify their strengths as readers, areas for improvement, and the strategies they found most helpful before, during, and after reading.

GRADE 7

(*The Ontario Curriculum, Grades 1-8*, revised, 2006)

What varies are the complexities of the expectations, the *suggested* types of resources, and modes of delivery. The more detailed grade 1 expectation 1.1 specifies that students are expected to "read a few different types of literary texts…, graphic texts…, and informational texts". The grade 7 expectation 1.1 notes that students should be able to "read a wide variety of increasingly complex or difficult texts from diverse cultures, including literary texts…, graphic texts…, and informational texts". See below for detailed examples.

SPECIFIC EXPECTATIONS

1. Reading for Meaning

By the end of Grade 1, students will:

Variety of Texts

1.1 read a few different types of literary texts (*e.g., pattern books, rhymes, books from home, simple fiction stories*), graphic texts (*e.g., calendars, environmental print, signs*), and informational texts (*e.g., morning messages, strategy charts, instructions, simple non-fiction books, labels*)

1. Reading for Meaning

By the end of Grade 7, students will:

Variety of Texts

1.1 read a wide variety of increasingly complex or difficult texts from diverse cultures, including literary texts (*e.g., short stories, poetry, novels, mysteries, historical fiction, autobiographies, scripts, lyrics*), graphic texts (*e.g., graphs and graphic organizers, charts and tables, diagrams, surveys, maps*), and informational texts (*e.g., print and online encyclopedias, manuals, and magazine and newspaper articles; magazines in their first languages, where appropriate; electronic texts, textbooks, and non-fiction materials; a variety of dictionaries, thesauri, and websites*)

Within this curriculum, there is much latitude to recognize voice and choice in the classroom and provide a variety of materials and resources that meet the needs of students in the classroom.

So I asked this question:

How might we bring the curriculum to life for students with varying interests and ways of learning?

The first and most straightforward answer to this question is to open the learning to resources beyond the classroom. I recall collecting class sets of books so that all my students could read the same text. I realize now how that well-intentioned action did not serve all my students. I didn't stop to think that all the students in grade 8 did not need to read *Hatchet* (Paulson, 1986) and all students in grade 3 did not need to read *Little House on the Prairie* (Wilder, 1935). More recently, I was surprised that my niece in grade 10 was reading *Romeo and Juliet* (Shakespeare, 1597) and *To Kill A Mockingbird* (Lee, 1960) in her high school English class — the same two texts I had read forty years earlier in grade 10. I realized that class set availability, or perhaps tradition, has continued to dominate reading selections at the expense of student voice and choice.

Voice and choice in the classroom mean:

- engaging students' interests and ideas;
- opening possibilities for classroom resources;
- creating and encouraging curriculum links between math and social studies, language and arts, science, health, and physical education; and
- facilitating alternate modes of demonstrating learning for assessment purposes.

Engaging Students' Interests and Ideas ✓

Sharing students' interests and ideas is where so many teachers find joy. This is where the "aha" moments arise. This is when growth on the part of the teacher and the student happens simultaneously. Without an understanding of students' ideas and interests, a teacher has limited capacity to effect meaningful change. Students who feel that the teacher does not know them well or is not interested in them as individuals lose their enthusiasm for participation in the classroom community, and as a result their interest in learning is diminished.

In a busy new classroom, start small. On the first day of the academic year, check in (see Action Strategy: Bringing It Back, p. 86) by asking each student to state their name and one topic they are particularly interested in. If you don't think you will remember, jot it down quickly as the sharing goes around the circle. On the second day, ask students a different question that requires only a brief answer, such as "Name your favorite place to be." On the third day, the check-in might be for students to share the name of their favorite song. By the end of the first week, the teacher should have some insights into who the students are and what their interests might be. Even if the teacher does not know each one's interests yet, a general awareness of class interest will be emerging. These little nuggets of information support relationship building as the teacher and the students begin to learn more about each person in the classroom. Some students may choose to pass in the conversation circle. The repeated choice to pass also provides insight by indicating who may need more care and attention while building trust and relationship.

With a general idea about where interests lie, teachers can begin to adapt the classroom and the curriculum to better meet the needs of the students. At first that might simply look like a baseball context for math problem solving, or time for a read-aloud on the grass in the schoolyard for a group that loves to be outdoors. Every step makes a difference. Students will come to realize that the teacher is listening to their voices and respecting their choices. The care and kindness shown will be reciprocated. Children have such great wisdom and sensitivity. When we listen to their voices, there is much to learn and much to gain.

THROUGH THE WINDOW...

If there's a good teacher there's good kids because you're treating them to be good. If not, hearts are getting shut and then they're being mean to other people and those people are being mean to other people, but if you're nice, then those people will be nice to other people and that person will be nice, too.

— V., age 8

Opening Possibilities for Classroom Resources ✓

THROUGH THE WINDOW...

In a grade 3 classroom where students were painting, the teacher had covered the desks with recycled newspaper for easy clean-up. Three students were gathered around one desk and engaged in quiet but excited conversation. As the teacher approached to speak to them about staying on task with their art, they directed her attention to a story in the newspaper about a polar bear that had wandered into the northern town. They had seen the photo and were busy helping each other to read the article for details. The teacher carefully cut out the article and put it in a plastic sleeve in the class reading basket so that others could read the article, too.

Many schools have a wide range of resources open to teachers. However, beyond the range offered by the school, teachers need to think outside the box to meet the needs of all students. Teachers can encourage the school librarian to include age-appropriate magazines in the library collection. Local newspapers may provide a few complimentary copies for the school. These are valuable even in the younger grades.

- An environmental print board can help young readers associate familiar word chunks to frequently used words in their writing. For example, a KitKat wrapper on an environmental print board helps children to read and spell any words containing "it" or "at". Soon children will be clamoring to add labels and will be using environmental print media to support their reading.
- A bulletin board near the classroom computers can serve as a spot to paste links to websites that students have found useful.

- A class visit to the school library might include time for the teacher to select a few books for the classroom library that will be rotated regularly, or invite volunteer class librarians to select two or three books for classroom use until the next library visit.
- Engagement in learning conversations that provide insights into the interests and the social issues that engage students also allows teachers to clip or print articles for the reading basket and encourages students to do likewise.
- Local bookstores likely maintain a list of new books that will enrich the classroom library. Parents who are gift-giving at holidays might consider books on the list that students could bring to school for a read-aloud or donate to the class library.
- Grocery or big box store flyers are great for linking math and language to health education and financial literacy.
- Cereal boxes provide opportunities for reading, analyzing text, and creating art as students design their own box, think about the influence of packaging on purchasing decisions, and learn how to read labels to ensure healthy choices.
- Short movies or film downloads that are relevant to class interests provide an opportunity for students to create their own endings. Show the movie/film until just before it ends. Ask students to create/write and share their own endings.
- A classroom library of student-created work allows other students to pick up a story or project written by a peer to learn more about a topic, or consider strategies used that will help them to make their own work stronger. Students who "publish" for the classroom library will make a greater effort to raise the level of their work.

ACTION STRATEGY: PUBLISHING

What…

Having an authentic audience who will appreciate their work affirms the importance and value of students' voices. Publishing can take many forms (books, websites, newspaper articles, letters to editors, etc.).

Implementation

How…

Beginning with realistic expectations about who, what, and how often your class will publish will make the process run more smoothly. Hardcover books can be created by a whole class collaboration or by small groups. To make a hardcover all you need is stiff cardboard, or discarded library book covers that can be re-covered with wallpaper or the self-adhesive plastic used to line drawers. The inner pages can be stapled then secured to the inside cover with duct tape. Classroom newsmagazines can be published per term. Classroom newspapers can be published monthly. With parental permission, letters to editors can be submitted to local papers. Publishing for young students can be supported by "Reading Buddies" in a higher grade. Alternatively, "Reading Buddies" could be encouraged to publish a story or an information text on a topic that interests their young reading partner.

Creating Cross-Curricular Links ✓

Creating cross-curricular links cuts a teacher's workload tremendously. Music is about fractions as students learn whole, half, and quarter notes. A song is a poem or a story set to music. Geometry is art and architecture in ancient and modern societies. Ratios and percentages are a study of demographics in a social studies curriculum. Podcasts require research and a written script and can be linked to any number of curriculum topics. Procedural writing records the details of a science experiment or accurately recording ingredients, measurements (math), and steps for a recipe. Counting down the clock in a basketball game facilitates understandings of number and time.

Integrating science, social studies, arts, and media into the math and literacy curriculum allows every lesson to do double duty. Linking a math or literacy lesson to the expectations of at least one other curriculum subject ensures curriculum is covered while engaging students in the learning. Virtually every lesson can be a math and/or literacy lesson coupled with other curricular content. Students can dribble basketballs in time to multiplication fact rhymes.

The following is just one example of how a little creativity enhanced the learning in the classroom.

The result of cross-curricular integration benefits both the teacher and the students who gain insight into the interconnectivity of their curricular learnings and their relevance to daily life. Literacy and numeracy live in almost all aspects of the curriculum. In a classroom where the community of students collaborate in activities across the curriculum, student engagement ensures successful learning.

Teacher Leadership ✓

Teachers as lead learners serve as both models and catalysts for student learning. Beyond the classroom, teachers can also be leaders within the school community. As experts in the complex world of teaching children, teachers have the opportunity to open their classroom doors within the school building and virtually within education forums to share practices, create informal professional learning communities, and mentor each other.

Have you implemented a new practice that is working well? Tell a colleague so that their students can benefit from your experience.

Struggling with differentiation or another strategy that sounds great when you read about it, but falls apart upon execution? Ask colleagues for advice and support. Try something new in the classroom while a colleague does likewise. Then compare notes to problem solve or fine tune the process.

Do you wish you had time to learn more about new education practices? Offer to mentor a teacher candidate in the classroom or support a first-year teacher. The mentoring process is a two-way exchange. It sparks new conversations about learning, creates a professional relationship that opens minds to different perspectives, and enlivens daily practice with new strategies and renewed enthusiasms for teaching.

With an interest in improving learning for your students and expanding your experience and learning as a teacher, you are already a leader. Think about the possibilities to reimagine your practice and seek out a colleague who will share the journey. Then collaboratively launch your "what if" thinking to lead each other into a new adventure in education.

5

Reimagining Learning for the 21st Century

I believe that each of us — student or teacher — is a mentor. We all have so much to learn from each other. Therefore, this chapter celebrates the ways in which we can **all** look to the future, support each other's learning, and collaborate to create new ways of thinking and being in the world. To do so, we must not only challenge "what is" in our classrooms, but visualize "what might be".

This book began with a story and so it will end, with the stories of three remarkable educators who have allowed me to share the "what if" thinking that transformed the learning experience for me and the students in our classrooms. In transforming student experience, these educators have made a difference.

Rhonda Robert was teaching in the classroom down the hall from mine. Our windows faced a hardscrabble plot in front of the school building. Within a school that needed resources and additional supports for students, there was no funding for improving a classroom view.

Noticing the amount of litter that had accumulated on a particularly windy day, we considered, "What if we got a few people together to clean it up?" The "what if" wondering blossomed into a student-built garden that stretched the length of the building. Rhonda created the vision and her father (a retired teacher) helped manage the project. He was a keen gardener and skilled carpenter. Together they developed a plan that included a garden to attract butterflies and a hexagonal bench around a tree so that classes could come out to read.

Parents donated perennial plants from their gardens. A local contractor offered some topsoil. Someone donated wood chips. Nevertheless, there was still much work to be done.

The Kindergarten students laid down old newspapers all over the existing space. My classroom had a window overlooking the soon-to-be garden, so students offered juice out of the "walk-through window", giving encouragement and appreciation to each class as they worked. Older students, with the help of parent volunteers, spread the soil evenly so others could begin planting. Finally, the grade 7 and 8 students covered the topsoil between the plants with wood chips.

The garden improved the view from the classrooms along the hallway, uplifted the front entry to the school, and created a quiet oasis under the big tree, where classes congregated for read-alouds. Students watched bees come to pollinate the flowers, and butterflies that flitted around. Every single child in the school could take pride in saying they had contributed to creating that garden. It was such a successful collaborative project that all began with "what if" thinking, and a group of enthusiastic teachers, parents, and students who believed that together they could make a difference.

* * *

Judy Blaney was teaching a course in Indigenous education at our university. One day she asked, "What if teacher candidates could do a teaching placement in an Indigenous community school?" There were immediate reasons why it couldn't happen. Not all students were free to travel, not all students had the financial means to travel, placements would be difficult to secure without pre-existing relationships with Indigenous communities, teacher candidates would be absent from all courses for that period, local teacher certification regulations might not recognize placements outside our area. It seemed that the logistical complexities would crush the pedagogical advantages.

With Judy at the helm, we took on the challenges. Indigenous communities and Friendship Centres within the local region welcomed teacher candidates closer to home to avoid long commutes. Teacher candidates and their families collaborated to ensure childcare and home support. For students who had the desire to travel, affordable homestays were arranged by families in Indigenous communities. Professors who had classes scheduled during the period agreed to accommodate students who would be absent from class with recognition of the unique and meaningful experience that teacher candidates would be undertaking. With the support of local Indigenous communities and school board leaders in Indigenous education, additional partnerships with communities beyond our immediate area were established. To prepare our teacher candidates to enter respectfully into Indigenous communities, local elders shared insights, experiences, and cultural perspectives that would ensure our teacher candidates were aware of the histories, perspectives, and current issues that impact First Nations, Métis, and Inuit peoples.

Years later, teacher candidates continue to bring the insights gained during the placement to students in their classrooms. Many have maintained professional relationships with Indigenous communities through correspondence, while others continue to work in Indigenous community schools. All were impacted by the learning. One "what if" idea continues to make a difference.

* * *

Natasha Marchant was a teacher candidate in the Faculty of Education program where I was teaching. The practice of Indigenous community placements was established by the time she entered the program. When looking at the placement sites, she asked, "What if we went to the far north to do placements in Nunavut?"

The familiar refrains echoed about funding, travel expense and distance, time away from classes, which would necessarily be extended due to the long travel, and the lack of existing community relationships in Nunavut. But within a group of "what if" thinkers, Natasha's vision of Arctic placements became a reality. Four teacher candidates signed up for the first year of the Arctic placement and I had the honor of accompanying them for a placement adjacent to the Arctic Circle.

The cultural learning from that experience remains for a lifetime. We worked in classrooms with children who had life skills that far exceeded our own. On a Kindergarten field trip out on the ice, we watched five-year-old children catch Arctic char to provide us with lunch. We witnessed the unique community spirit when children in a classroom shared a single orange or banana (a rare treat when all produce is flown in to the community) by cutting it into twenty pieces, one for every member of the class.

I recall sitting with a young child to support his reading. I was busy asking questions, and quite surprised that the child was not responding. Imagine my embarrassment when I was kindly advised that traditional indications of yes (raised eyebrows and open eyes) and no (wrinkled nose) were escaping my notice. Indeed, the young learner was responding to my questions but I was unaware of the meaning of his responses. I immediately wondered how a child might feel marginalized coming to a classroom in my town with a teacher who did not understand the importance of sharing a piece of fruit with the class or the subtle signals of traditional communication. I determined that I would learn more, raise my awareness, and recognize how little I knew. In how I live, teach, and think about ways of knowing and being in the world today, the experience made a difference.

So I asked this question:

How might we reimagine learning for the 21st century in simple ways that make a difference to student thinking and learning?

Through the power of the internet and social media, students can learn, ask questions, wonder about possibilities, dream about new ways of doing and being in the world, and have their voices heard by a wider audience than we would ever have thought possible only a few years ago. On the other hand, education today is challenged by many problems that include inadequate funding, less than ideal physical environments, staffing shortages, societal inequities, and conflicting philosophies. While new strategies have emerged that have been heralded as game changers, they too often become another bandwagon that educators are expected to jump up on, only to be told a few years later that what we have been doing is all wrong. Yet as I see it, the potential for change is greater than ever before. By facilitating and supporting a new generation of learners who are innovative thinkers as well as effective communicators and collaborators, the potential to make a difference is truly beyond imagination.

For students to become the learners and thinkers who will create a healthy and vibrant tomorrow, we must all learn to think in new ways. This begins with questioning the understanding or misunderstanding that curriculum defines the work of the classroom. In conversations about teachers, how often do we hear a teacher identified or defined by the grade, subject, or level they teach? Alex is the English teacher. Evelyn is the grade 4 teacher. A simple refocus on what is at the heart of teaching can make a big difference. What if there was a conscious movement to articulate that teachers teach students? Of course, teachers know that already, but what if it began to be *enough* to say I teach children/adolescents/ teacher candidates — to make it explicit that above and beyond all else, beyond curriculum expectations, teachers teach learners? Returning to Vygotsky's idea that "Thought is not merely expressed in words; it comes into existence through them" (*Thought and Language,* 1934/1986), perhaps by articulating our belief that children are at the heart of our teaching, we can ensure that the words bring into existence a new way of looking at learning.

What if we thought about what is really important for the children we teach, for tomorrow's leaders? What do they actually need? What is of true importance to their success in the future?

I believe that children need to understand the importance of **well-being** to their learning, their personal lives, and the lives of everyone in their community. They need to understand and celebrate the value of **citizenship** and their ability to take responsibility as citizens of the world, their country, and their community. They need an understanding of their responsibility for **stewardship** in caring for society and this planet we call home, and in finding innovative ways to make it better, so that generations to come will also have a home. Finally, I believe that children need to have an awareness of the power of the **legacy** that they leave to the next generation, and their ability to make the world a better place.

Ensuring that students have these understandings does not mean throwing curriculum out the window. Of course, students need to learn language(s) — to read, write, listen, articulate, and create. They need to explore science, examine history, and celebrate arts. They need an understanding of mathematics and exposure to literature. However, I ask:

- ✓ "*What if* the core values of well-being, citizenship, stewardship, and legacy become the foundation, with the curriculum expectations acting simply as the tools that teachers and students use to create deeper meaning and understanding of their world?
- ✓ *What if* teachers embedded curriculum in authentic, relevant, meaningful, and purposeful learning engagements that facilitated students seeing themselves as valuable, responsible, caring, and forward-thinking members of both a local and a global community?

I know that many teachers are already undertaking activities that lead students to an understanding of their importance in the world. No doubt, others are doing this but simply not naming it in the classroom. So, what if we open some doors to witness how overarching values of well-being, citizenship, stewardship, and legacy can become the source from which curriculum naturally flows?

Well-Being

Well-being incorporates the mental and physical health of an individual. While physical health refers to the state of an individual's body, mental health refers to the state of an individual's emotions, mind, and feelings. A student's ability to learn successfully will be greatly impacted by their well-being. The inextricable link between successful learning and student well-being necessitates awareness on the part of teachers from the earliest grades.

A key factor in student well-being is resilience. Resilience refers to the individual's ability to cope with the inevitable challenges that arise in life. Students who learn strategies to deal with the issues that they face strengthen their resilience and are better prepared to address additional challenges in life.

- Positivity in the classroom, a "can-do" attitude on the part of teachers and students, and understanding that learning is complex and requires patience and perseverance will support students when the going gets tough.
- Providing windows into your own thinking and things you do to deal with stress demonstrates to young students that they have the power to help themselves. Working directly with students to help them develop resilience and coping mechanisms will support them greatly as they learn.

The Center on the Developing Child at Harvard University (2023) identifies four key factors that optimize resilience:

- facilitating supportive adult-child relationships,
- building a sense of self-efficacy and perceived control;
- providing opportunities to strengthen adaptive skills and self-regulatory capacities; and
- mobilizing sources of faith, hope, and cultural traditions. (https://developingchild.harvard.edu/science/key-concepts/resilience/)

So I asked this question:

How might we enhance students' well-being and resilience through classroom learning?

Prior chapters have discussed strategies for relationship building between teacher and student and within the classroom community. In the classroom, the general perception is that the supportive element of the relationship flows from teacher to student. However, when the classroom dynamic provides students with an understanding that relationships are reciprocal and equitable, it can be empowering for the students and affirming for the teacher.

THROUGH THE WINDOW...

My classroom had a big bulletin board that said, "Welcome to the Happy Class". It was decorated with happy face cutouts. The students took to referring to themselves as "The Happy Class" and holiday gifts from students included much happy face paraphernalia, including a pair of large, fluffy, yellow happy face slippers.

One day, noticing my frustration with a classroom situation, a student went to our classroom cupboard and took out the slippers. As she brought them to me she said, "Mrs. Vetter, I think you need your happy slippers right now." It was both a thoughtful and an insightful gesture.

As I put on the slippers I realized how much these children had learned about taking control of emotions and frustrations before they got out of hand and interfered with our learning. I also realized that the sense of responsibility for the well-being of the classroom extended to everyone in our classroom community, including the teacher.

> Those slippers eventually wore out and were no longer bright yellow, but I often think of them when the frustrations of life reach into my soul. I imagine putting on the slippers and the sincerity of that child's face. It was a real lesson to me in the power of simple kindness and of self-regulation.

It is important to recognize that children have a vast capacity for empathy and for support of their peers and the adults in their world. Welcoming their thoughtful and empathetic gestures demonstrates to them that the relationship is truly reciprocal and that they can make a difference in their world.

Self-efficacy describes the confidence that we hold in our ability to control our behavior, our motivations to act and succeed, and our social sphere. Research argues that confidence is a result of both nature and nurture; therefore, students may come to the classroom with a sense of confidence or a lack thereof. Providing every child with opportunities to have their voice heard and valued and to succeed in classroom pursuits will not change a child's inherent nature but will allow that child to develop greater belief in their ability to succeed. Likewise, supporting students in feeling secure and respected within the classroom community helps them develop their personal motivations and perceive themselves as able to influence their environment.

THROUGH THE WINDOW...

A grade 6 class began the new year with a rich vocabulary of four-letter words. Perhaps it was attributable to greater exposure to "grown-up" music and media, or perhaps it was just coming of age. Nevertheless, an intervention was required. The resulting conversation was based on respect rather than judgment. It also focused on the power of language and challenged students to find adjectives, adverbs, and expressions of amazement or awe that replaced expletives. It was quite a treat to hear some of the "stupendously" or "horrifically" articulate expressions they created.

Added to the list of "not-in-the-classroom" four-letter words was "can't". At first it was funny as students admonished each other for swearing when someone said "can't". However, it soon caught on that replacing "I can't do this", with "I need some help to do this", or "Do you have any ideas about how I could do this?" changed an unsuccessful attempt at a task into a successful one.

Often the mere thought of a task or new learning seems overwhelming to students. They don't know where to begin and they don't see a light at the end of the tunnel. Having each student keep a notebook or journal of questions, key strategies, and graphic or visual reminders can help them anchor their learning and organize their work. This makes launching and sustaining a new task much easier. The "Anchor Book" becomes a personalized self-help book to guide students as they begin a new task.

ACTION STRATEGY: ANCHOR BOOKS

What...

Teachers are likely familiar with Anchor Charts on classroom walls that hold ideas, strategies, and questions that lead learning so that they don't drift away from students' consciousness. An Anchor Book works in much the same way, but it is personalized to a student's needs. Begin by engaging students in a discussion of questions. How might asking questions make me think more deeply? How might asking questions make my work easier? What strategies are helpful to me? Once students begin to see the value of recording personalized questions and strategies or reminders to learn, they will see their Anchor Book as a useful tool.

Implementation

How...

Each student uses a notebook or binder to create a personalized collection of anchor strategies that help them to learn. Strategies can be accompanied by student drawings to facilitate understanding. For example, young students might draw a chain to remind them to make connections, or draw a TV to remind them to visualize when they are reading. Anchor Books are not divided by subject. Rather, they are organized by learning skill — strategies that help students to read across the curriculum; to improve their writing; to create stronger questions to support inquiry and critical thinking; and to listen effectively to the perspectives and ideas of others. A few pages may be set aside for new words to enhance writing, or feelings about successfully completing a task that will help to motivate the start of a subsequent task. There might be a grammar section to help students remember spellings of difficult words or the difference between "then" and "than".

Why...

Students who work their way through the elementary grades through memorization and surface understanding of *what*, and perhaps *how*, but never build deep understandings of *why* or *what if* in their learning, will find that learning in secondary school is greatly challenging. Learning how to learn and thinking metacognitively about the ways of learning that work most effectively is a key skill to successful lifelong learning. The Anchor Book gives students control over their learning and asks them to think about the strategies that help them learn.

What If...

What if students used their Anchor Books as evidence of how they can control and motivate their own learning? Starting a new school year might be less stressful with a reminder of prior year successes and reminders of key strategies that can be reapplied.

Some students choose to use their Anchor Books as a journal, too. Reading how they felt prior to starting a story or project and how they felt after it was done can be helpful to keep students motivated. Questions can be specific to the issue or subject of the inquiry, such as "How do bees make honey?" or related to a specific task-based goal that can be applied to any similar task, such as "How do I want my reader to feel reading my story?" or "How can I make my work interesting?"

The Anchor Book is cross-curricular. Students can have a page or two set aside for expressive new words that enhance their writing, strategies that help them to read (make connections, visualize, etc.), or anything else they feel will be of value to them. The Anchor Book addresses the specific needs of each student and is their own personal collection of support mechanisms.

This strategy can also work well for younger children who will record their thinking in words and pictures. The Anchor Book initiates their thinking about taking responsibility for their learning. As students begin to use their Anchor Books more often, they come to prize the content as a personal memento of their progress, rather like a scrapbook. In some cases, students have kept their Anchor Book from the prior year and brought it to a new classroom to set them off on the right foot.

Self-regulation differs from self-efficacy in that self-regulation is a control mechanism to rein in disruptive behaviors, calm tempers or anxieties, and restore an inner sense of harmony. Children learn early the "stop, drop, and roll" protocol to protect their bodies in case clothing catches fire. It is therefore logical to teach them to "stop, think, and breathe" when minds are spinning out of control.

THROUGH THE WINDOW...

During the Covid pandemic, I spent a lot of time with my four-year-old grandson. We often did yoga. It required little equipment or space, and we enjoyed the time together. Once schools were back in session, we heard from the daycare centre that when another child was feeling upset and anxious, my grandson brought two chairs to the window and sat with the child to breathe and calm his concerns.

Stopping to focus on breathing (breathing in to a count of four then breathing out to a count of four) is a simple form of self-regulation. Other techniques take a little more focus but are very effective. Square breathing (breathe in for a count of four, hold for a count of four, breathe out for a count of four, rest for a count of four), for instance, is another viable method.

While we focus on rhythmic breathing, heart rates go down, stress decreases, the nervous system begins to calm, and there is a shift in energy that can clear thinking. The benefit of rhythmic breathing is that it can be done anywhere and any time. If a classroom or a group of students is becoming overwhelmed by a situation or incident, the teacher can model the strategy by asking students to stop and breathe together. Once this strategy becomes embedded in classroom routine, students can undertake it independently when and as needed.

Self-regulation is an important skill for students in a classroom community. There are a number of self-regulation strategies to support student learning and enhance classroom harmony. Encouraging students to pause and regulate emotions and behaviors when stressed may prevent outbursts that lead to the disruption of all students.

Most children adopt a favorite toy, blanket, thumb, or other item to help them self-regulate when the going gets tough. Although such items are not usually seen in the classroom, for young learners they continue to be a source of comfort or strength at home. Older students and adults find that a stress reliever is a valuable tool.

To help students draw on this strategy in the classroom, a small smooth pebble works well. Worry stones used to be popular and this is a variation on that theme.

At the beginning of the year, students can choose a small smooth pebble from a basket. Pebbles are usually available by the bagful in dollar stores or from a landscape or garden centre. If teachers have access to a stream or river, hand-collected stones may provide greater meaning to students.

ACTION STRATEGY: HAPPY SLIPPERS TOOLKIT

What...

Noticing my frustration one day with a classroom situation, a student went to our classroom cupboard and took out a pair of large, yellow, fluffy, happy-face slippers that had been given to me as a gift. The student brought me the slippers and said, "Mrs. Vetter, I think you need your happy slippers right now." She was right! I have come to think of self-regulation strategies as my "happy slippers" toolkit. It is just one of many ways to recognize, reduce, and then reflect on stress to restore energy (Shankar/The Mehrit Center, 2022). There is a wide range of actions that can reduce stress in the classroom and help students to self-regulate and refocus on learning, including deep breathing, focusing on an object, or stepping away physically or virtually.

Implementation

How...

Teachers can facilitate self-regulation by actively naming and modeling strategies that students can use to de-escalate stressful situations. When noise levels rise, rather than ask students to be quiet, teachers use a soft voice to suggest that everyone take a pause to breathe deeply and focus on the task at hand. In a classroom with a central focus design, the teacher can remind students to stop and reflect using a central table item as the focal point that draws the mind and the stress away from a situation. A soothing item such as a small smooth pebble can help students to work away frustrations by visualizing pebbles in a stream or hearing the soothing sound of water running in a brook. After a gym class or active recess, a few moments of quiet music can help racing minds and hearts get back to learning mode.

Why...

Shankar (2022) reminds both parents and educators that stress impacts learning at many levels and advocates for seeking ways to reframe behavior, recognize the stressors, reduce the stress, reflect to enhance stress awareness, and restore energy, noting that when a child's central control system for stress becomes overwhelmed, the child has difficulty staying focused and alert, which is the optimal state for learning.

What If...

What if our lesson plans made explicit the expectations for student well-being in addition to student learning? Knowing that optimal learning requires focused and alert students, it makes sense to consider the stressors that impact our students (excessive noise, learning challenges, social interactions, academic pressures, or interpersonal relationships) and work towards a classroom plan that facilitates self-regulation and brings a sense of calm to the mind, body, and classroom.

This strategy is best launched by searching out a YouTube or video clip of water running over rocks and showing it in the classroom. As the students watch the video they can hold their pebble in the palms of their hands, feel how smooth it is.

Then they can feel how the water has worn away the sharp edges. The teacher can lead the students in a visualization as they listen to the running water and imagine the calm feeling of dipping fingers and toes into the cool stream. Together teacher and students can imagine moving from feeling hot and tired from running on a sunny day to cool and refreshed by the moving water. Children have wonderful imaginations and they will take to this visualization far more quickly than adults. A gentle reminder to put "Rocky" in their palm and think of the running water when frustrations arise soon becomes a mental exercise that calms students in the classroom.

Much research has been done on the topic of self-regulation. Students who learn to self-regulate demonstrate greater success in learning and, as long-range studies have shown, in life.

Having one strategy that works for everyone may be unrealistic. The key is to find strategies that you are comfortable sharing with your students and they are comfortable using. Different students will find that different strategies work for them. The important piece is that everyone has a strategy at their fingertips when conflicts erupt or stress rises.

Once students get used to taking responsibility for their learning and self-regulation, they can use the learned strategies to calm concerns or stress about learning, classroom dynamics, and tasks or issues that may seem daunting. As a result, the classroom community becomes a kinder and gentler place. Students come to understand that nobody "makes them angry", they choose to get angry. They could have chosen to use their pebble or their breathing strategies instead. Empathy for others grows as students realize that everyone has moments when they feel overwhelmed or tired. Instead of name calling when someone hurts their feelings, students turn to wonder, asking themselves what might have caused another child to be unkind. They will learn to gently remind each other that it is okay to stop, think, and breathe. Others may bring their pebble to a sad classmate in a show of solidarity. In a classroom that welcomes students' voices, this type of supportive talk between classmates sustains the community. When students make use of the strategies, be sure to affirm their wise and healthy choices. The ongoing affirmations will help them to make good choices the next time, too.

When students are feeling low or slide into "not learning" modes, reminders of how they felt when they started a prior project and how they prevailed helps develop feelings of hope for a good outcome and faith in their ability to succeed. A bulletin board of photos showcasing proud students holding up completed art, stories, or research projects celebrates the community's endeavors and emphasizes the value of the community. Those photos can act as reminders that resilience and perseverance have rewards. Soon you will see students adopting supportive talk to mentor each other. Children will learn from and emulate what teachers model and mentor in the classroom.

Finally, ensure the students have plenty of time to move. Take a seventh-inning stretch regularly to let bodies and minds take a pause. Take advantage of gym time to get everyone moving. Find constructive ways to hold children accountable for their disruptive actions, rather than implementing penalties that keep them indoors at recess or have them miss time in the gym. Children who are acting out need more time, not less, to move and expend their excess energy and emotion. Head outdoors for learning when weather permits. Think outside the box to consider what learning the schoolyard holds. Physical and mental health go hand in hand to ensure student well-being and successful learning. Nurturing a classroom community supports student well-being and is foundational to higher-level thinking and deeper engagement in and commitment to learning.

Citizenship

The world has seen innumerable challenges in recorded history. Wars, famines, natural disasters, and human-created catastrophes have impacted lives forever. In the past, history has recorded people uniting against a common challenge. Today, it seems that global challenges have raised animosities, divisiveness, and self-interest that scream for rights yet overlook responsibility. I wonder if (and hope that) this is only a perception that is fueled by headlines, since kindness and humanity rarely make the news.

So I asked this question:

How might we help students to embrace their roles and responsibilities as citizens, both locally and globally?

Learning about our roles and responsibilities as citizens stretches across every aspect of the curriculum. There is no shortage of reading material or opportunities for the production of text, video, voice, art, music, poetry, and media to gain insights and share understandings. Mathematics, science, engineering, and technology inhabit conversations about citizenship in everything from community planning and road construction to population and charitable pursuits. Consider how many examples from your community could be used to teach ratios to a grade 7 class: parks to coffee shops by number, parks to coffee shops by square area; small business to big box stores, and more.

In the primary grades, a simple walk around the block in the school community will demonstrate to young learners that numerals are used in many differing ways: house numbers, licence plates, prices, billboards, speed limits, posters, thermometers, parking meters, parking signs for different times of day, clocks, and sports jerseys. Plants, trees, birds, and bugs in parks or rural areas hold a wealth of opportunities for exploration. The shapes of buildings demonstrate the importance of geometry and structures. There are countless curriculum-linked ways to engage students in thinking about their communities and in citizenship learning within their community. Once you begin to think of them, they will seem to keep popping up at you wherever you go. Here are a few suggestions to launch the learning:

Embrace the Calls to Action for Educators (Government of Canada, Reconciliation for Educators, 2021).

https://www.rcaanc-cirnac.gc.ca/eng/1524504501233/1557513602139

September 1st, 2021, marked the first National Day for Truth and Reconciliation in Canada. Based on the 94 "Calls to Action" determined by the Truth and Reconciliation Commission (TRC, 2015), Canadians are called each year to recommit to implementing the actions. For those in education, Calls to Action 62, 63, 64, and 65 focus on the work to be done by policy makers "in consultation and collaboration with Survivors, Aboriginal Peoples and educators…to provide leadership, funding, curriculum, resources, teaching training and best practices, and a national research program". Of particular importance to the conversation about students mentoring each other through communication, collaboration, and community, Call to Action 63 (iii) specifically calls for "Building student capacity for intercultural understanding, empathy and mutual respect".

As educators, we have a responsibility to educate even our youngest citizens on the importance of recognition of, and responsibility for, reconciliation in ways that respect and uphold the Calls to Action, which specifically mention learning for K–12. There is a wealth of children's literature written by Indigenous authors that provides young children with the opportunity to develop their understandings of Indigenous histories, perspectives, ways of knowing, and current concerns. A Reuters news article from August 2022 noted that a 12-pack of soft drink cans sold for $27 in Nunavut. Fresh fruit and vegetables are extremely expensive. Those facts could launch a math lesson comparing prices in your community to a northern community, a geography lesson considering the impact of weather, road access, and location on the delivery of goods to remote locations, a history lesson, and much more.

Recognize the value of challenging conversations.

It is often suggested that students in the elementary grades are not ready to discuss challenging social issues. I certainly agree that conversations must be age-appropriate. However, many social issues are addressed effectively in children's picture books. The reality of our schools today is that many children have personal experience with societal issues of great importance that merit conversation. In addition, young learners working together scaffold learning by witnessing and building on each other's thinking. Curriculum topics are easily linked to social issues: For example, Energy > Climate Change; Life Systems > Food Insecurity; Literacy Expectations > Homelessness; Science > Sustainability and Biodiversity.

Teachers may wonder about the advisability of connecting to social justice issues for fear of exposing students to elements that may unsettle them. However, the reality is that issues such as food insecurity, homelessness, and racism may have a daily presence in the lives of our students. Discussing issues that impact local families does not have to create fear. Just the opposite, it has the potential to create empathy and the opportunity for students to see themselves as capable of making a difference in the world. Empathy is created through understanding the perspective of another. Mentoring partnerships encourage the development of empathy for the experience of another.

My students' ability to embrace conversations about social justice issues and their ability to visualize themselves as having the power to "make the world a better place" (Vetter, 2008) taught me that young students are ready to discuss social issues when those issues are put in context with their experience and understanding of the world. Reflecting on social issues and engaging in conversations about social justice as catalysts for learning through communication, collaboration, and community-building inspire understanding and help students become rational yet innovative thinkers whose first question is, "How can I make a difference?"

Mother Teresa is reported to have said, "We cannot all do great things, but we can do small things with great love". We do not need to present students with the overwhelming task of saving the world, simply the task of making a difference today, even for just one other person. What a great way to teach exponents to students in the upper elementary grades. If I do something to make a difference to two people, and they both do something to make a difference to two people, where might it lead? The story of *Ordinary Mary's Extraordinary Deed* (Pearson, 2002) is a good example of kindness that grows. It illustrates the point quite clearly and introduces exponents. A math lesson on exponents can act as a catalyst for undertaking class projects or actions to make a difference within the classroom, the school, and the community.

THROUGH THE WINDOW...

A grade 4 class read *Dear Children of the Earth* (Schimmel, 1994), a beautifully illustrated text that imagines Mother Earth writing to the children of the world. Following the reading, the class wrote back to Mother Earth with their thoughts, ideas, and intentions. The letters were so well-written that the teacher invited the students to create a podcast that was shared with families and spurred many interesting at-home conversations.

If children are provided with the opportunity to engage critically with current issues that exist in the world around them and, importantly, are shown that their voices are valued and respected, they will develop the ability to discern injustice and the confidence to speak out about social issues. In doing so, they will be building a foundation of global awareness, from which they may begin the process of becoming concerned and informed global citizens.

Explore innovative thinking.

What begins in wonder is learned in earnest.
— Richard Wagamese, 2019

I recall visiting a teacher candidate placed in a school that valued innovative thinking. The lesson that day focused on biomimicry. The students were studying the properties of burrs that stick to our clothes after a walk in the woods and drive us crazy as we attempt to disengage them from socks, mittens, and pant legs. The teacher provided the grade 5 students with an opportunity to inquire into the similarities between burrs and Velcro. I distinctly remember walking away from the observation of that lesson in an "oh wow" frame of mind.

The students in the classroom were learning about nature as part of their science curriculum, but they were also learning about innovative thinking and how the properties of a naturally occurring entity might be put into service to enhance daily living. This example has remained with me as I consider the difference between teaching by the curriculum and teaching for future innovation through curriculum. What a gift to the children in that grade 5 classroom to be exposed to such relevant examples of science and how the properties of nature might be used to create new and wondrous products or technologies for tomorrow.

ACTION STRATEGY: WONDER WALLS

What…

A unique way to encourage students to lead the development of innovative thinking is a Wonder Wall. Wonder Walls are simply bulletin boards, or chart papers, on which students can share their questions and wonderings about classroom topics. I recall a presenter showing us a photo of a Wonder Wall on which a young student had written "I wndr hw my ski staz on" ["I wonder how my skin stays on"]. A classmate had followed up with a question that translated to "I wonder why my eyes don't fall out". I would have loved to see the Wonder Wall at the end of the week as each child mentored the next in demonstrating the power of wonder and innovative thinking.

In the example above, the class was beginning a unit on the human body. The Wonder Wall encourages students to add their own wonderings in which one thought generally begets or builds upon another. It is always interesting to see the path that wondering takes in the classroom, and the enthusiasm for learning that builds as the list of wonderings grows.

Implementation

How…

The Wonder Wall is easy to create with a piece of chart paper on a stand or taped to a wall where students can easily reach to write their wonderings. A handy basket of washable markers allows students to write freely and protect walls if the writing goes off or through the paper. The most important thing is that the Wonder Wall is visible by and accessible to all students in the classroom. It is not a place where spelling is corrected. Students need to feel free to add whatever wonderings they have without concern if they don't know how to spell a word. No *wondering* is wrong!

Why…

The Wonder Wall becomes the jumping-off point for study of a new unit of curriculum. It serves as a catalyst to spur student thinking about new topics of study and generates enthusiasm for learning as students begin to contemplate what they are keen to learn about the area of study. Wonder Walls also provide insight for teachers into the thinking of students, allowing teachers to facilitate deeper thinking and cognitive development. Wonder Walls in the youngest grades help students develop an understanding that wondering and questioning are foundational to all learning. Students who wonder and question develop stronger learning skills.

What If…

What if students were prompted to seek wonderings and questions rather than correct answers? What if the explorations and inquiries that evolve from wonderings were celebrated more so than the results? Where would we be today if Galileo had not wondered about the stars?

Stewardship and Legacy

> A society grows great when old men plant trees in whose shade they shall never sit.
> — Greek proverb

This well-known proverb contains much wisdom; however, it causes me to wonder if the writer intended to convey that tree planting, as an analogy for stewardship of the future, lies solely in the purview of old men.

So I asked the question:

How might we inspire young students to greet the present with an eye to caring for the world they will live in as adults, and to think of the legacy that they are building?

In our district, the Kindergarten curriculum includes expectations that classroom activities will "lay the foundations for citizenship and environmental stewardship" (Ontario Ministry of Education, 2016) and support children's sense of belonging and contributing through collaboration, empathy, and inclusiveness. These expectations are ideally addressed through collaborative activities that allow students to share learnings and learning experiences.

So many of our students are stressed today, some by struggles and challenges, others by pressures to excel and succeed, and many by concern for their well-being or societal demands. Imagine the potential impact of allowing these students to engage with a moment that has no cost or demands, only benefits to their wellness and a resultant impact on their learning. Students study photosynthesis and the importance of trees to the production of oxygen. Ensuring outdoor learning time supports the curriculum, enhances student well-being, and reminds students of the responsibility we all have to sustain the ecosystems of the planet.

THROUGH THE WINDOW...

A friend who is a recently retired teacher has launched a local business leading guided tree bathing excursions. At first I was a bit unsure of what this was all about. However, receiving reassurance from my friend that it had nothing to do with actually taking a bath in the woods, I was encouraged to participate in an extraordinary experience. Originating in Japan, the concept is to *bathe* or *immerse oneself* in the calm of the forest. Research on the practice of forest bathing has demonstrated significant benefits to both physical and mental well-being.

I loved the experience of forest bathing and considered how simple it would be to gather a group of students under a tree in the schoolyard, or in a local park, to partake in the experience and the emanating wellness.

It is important for everyone to understand the value of getting outdoors and refreshing their brain power. As the classroom begins to work as a cohesive community and collaborates on projects, the issue becomes those who want to remain indoors during a break. When students are engaged in a community project, taking a recess break often seems like a disruption. Some fresh air during recess or classroom breaks revives the body and soul for students and teachers alike. Photocopying can wait…you might even find it wasn't necessary after all.

ACTION STRATEGY: NATURE NURTURES

What…

The premise is embedded in research on eco-therapy. Livni (2016) notes, "…science has proven that time in nature lowers heart rate and blood pressure, reduces stress hormone production, boosts the immune system, and improves overall feelings of wellbeing".

This strategy is based on the Japanese practice of "shinrin-yoku" or "bathing in the forest atmosphere". In this case, bathing means immersing oneself in the environment, not literally taking a bath. The Nature Nurtures strategy has two objectives. Firstly, it encourages students and teachers to move learning outdoors more often … a local forest, a neighborhood park, or simply the schoolyard. Secondly, this strategy encourages schools to consider the value of adding trees to playground areas and making use of space on all four sides of the school to create safe outdoor learning spaces. There is often an expanse of grass between the school and the road. With some creative thinking that space could be repurposed to support outdoor learning.

Implementation

How…

Begin by googling Outdoor Education in your local school district. Many government agencies, outdoor education centres, and teacher organizations have terrific online resources that will help you move learning outdoors. Take it one step at a time. The expectation is not to remake your classroom program, but simply to add more outdoor learning time each week. If you are looking to begin with a resource that offers a selection of ideas to choose from, try accessing http://www.metrovancouver.org/events/school-programs/K12publications/GetOutdoors.pdf, or a similar resource. A number of online guides contain activities for K–12 classrooms with plenty of entry points for teachers new to taking it outdoors.

Why…

Although research on young children is sparse, extensive research on the impact of being in nature on adults and adolescents demonstrates a reduction of stress and an enhancement of health, both physical and mental, as a result of increased outdoor time and activity.

What If…

What if reframing the way we do things in the classroom moved from addressing the challenges to considering the possibilities? How might we change just one thing in our learning program to move outdoors just once a week? Thinking beyond recess, which often seems chaotic, how might we plan outdoor activities that inspire, calm, and renew student energy and enthusiasm for learning?

When we think of stewardship, the initial inclination is to consider the environment. However, the concept of stewardship is not limited to trees, the ocean, or the environment. The dictionary lists the definition of stewardship as "the careful and responsible management of something entrusted to one's care" (Merriam-Webster, 2022). Rising to this challenge of stewardship of children's learning requires much forward thinking.

No doubt every teacher joined the world in grieving when the space shuttle Challenger exploded shortly after liftoff in 1986 with teacher Christa McAuliffe on board. Ms. McAuliffe stated in a pre-flight interview that she wanted to bring her "wonder and excitement back to students". She continued, "We see the space program as a science or math or technological adventure right now. I want the students to get a little bit of ownership. I want them to feel that they're part of the space age because they're the future" (*Today*, 1985).

Thirty-five years later, in 2021, Blue Origin's sub-orbital spaceflights had the opportunity to bring students virtually to the border of outer space. There was such great potential for these flights to enlighten and inspire student learning about space and venturing beyond our current understandings. Yet the educative opportunities were overshadowed by the marketing hype of taking Captain Kirk (actor William Shatner) to space. What a missed opportunity to inspire young scientists, pioneers, and explorers!

Stewardship of tomorrow's great thinkers requires inspiration by today's leaders in business, science, and technology. It also requires students to visualize and celebrate the work that they can do in the community and the classroom to make a difference. Vasquez (2004/2014) engaged Kindergarten learners in celebrating their inquiries by creating a physical trail of their thoughts, inquiries, artefacts, conclusions, and wonderings on the classroom walls. Vasquez called these "audit trails". I consider them to be a representation of students' thinking journeys. When students have tangible proof of their work and celebrations of their success they are inspired to continue to learn and explore.

ACTION STRATEGY: THINKING JOURNEYS

What…

The Thinking Journey is a visual representation of the work of the classroom in studying a particular issue and/or its related curriculum links. The Thinking Journey includes artifacts, pictures, thoughts, ideas, and documentation of how the study began and evolved over a period of time. The Thinking Journey provides documentation of learning for parents, teachers, and students.

Implementation

How…

Within an integrated unit of study that includes multiple cross-curricular objectives and is linked to an issue that is authentic and meaningful to students' interests and understandings, the students and teacher collect artefacts, photos, drawings, ideas, and links that document the learning and thinking that students have undertaken during their inquiry. All the documentation is displayed on the classroom wall to facilitate a "walk through" of the study. The Thinking Journey is a visual celebration of the work and wonderings of the classroom, which allows students to see the progress in their thinking and learning from the beginning of the study.

Why…

The process of learning, particularly in the elementary grades, provides students with a roadmap for learning in the future. Documenting the initial wonderings, the process of investigation and inquiry, the steps taken to gain deeper understandings, the resources gathered, and the collaborative effort of the class helps students to internalize not only the learning but the process of learning and what has helped them to learn effectively. In addition, the celebration of the learning through the visual display generates enthusiasm for future inquiries.

What If…

What if the goal at the end of each school day was to celebrate the day's learning? What if students understood each day to be a milestone in learning, rather than a millstone that feels burdensome?

Consider the walls of the classroom. What might they reflect of student learning and thinking? Are they examples of the best of student product or evidence of student thinking? Product is neat and often visually appealing. Thinking can be messy and imprecise. Nevertheless, the opportunity to see their thinking displayed, along with the artefacts that inspired that thinking, helps students to internalize understandings and reflect on what they did, what they might have done differently, and what their next steps might be.

* * *

Every profession has the opportunity to impact the future, but I would argue that none has greater potential than teaching. Each of us has the power to inspire the greatest minds of tomorrow. We may never know we have done so, but the sparks of learning and engagement that begin in our classrooms may ignite change and innovation for the future. My father always said, "Be aware of what you say and do, as your name will go where your feet will never take you." This is especially true for teachers. I know that my own children loved to quote their teachers, then remind me, "Mom, you don't know. You are not *my* teacher."

Over the years, I have had the privilege of welcoming thousands of new teacher candidates to the faculty of education. I usually ask them to first think of the very best teacher they have ever had in their years of schooling, perhaps a teacher who made a big difference in their lives or spurred them on to become teachers. In a large auditorium, students call out words that describe these teachers. Here are some words I have frequently heard:

• Caring	• Positive	• Friendly
• Empathetic	• Encouraging	• Helpful
• Kind	• Funny	• Reliable
• Patient	• Supportive	• Real
• Empowering	• Collaborative	• Trusting
• Interested	• Open-minded	• Concerned
• Engaging	• Respectful	• Truthful

In all the years of undertaking this activity, I rarely hear words such as "knowledgeable" or "intelligent". In discussing this with teacher candidates, it seems that, indeed, the best teachers may be intelligent and knowledgeable, but these are not the descriptors that make the deepest impression on their students. What matters most to learners are the qualities that nurture the student as a learner and create an environment that invites the student to learn. As teacher educators, we can teach our new teachers to effectively plan a lesson, set up a classroom, and assess and evaluate learning. The *nuts and bolts* (lesson planning, differentiated instruction, etc.) are relatively easy to teach to those new to the profession. Yet the qualities that are most important to students are ones that we need to rely on new teachers to bring with them as they enter the profession. So we must model for them, mentor them, and help them to value these qualities so that they might bring them to their own classrooms to nurture, support, affirm, and value the great minds of tomorrow.

This brings me to the final Action Strategy for this book, which is a favorite in demonstrating the understanding that what we do is richer for the collaboration and support that we bring to our collective learning.

Based on Stone Soup, which is a traditional European folktale where a group of strangers tell sceptical villagers they can make a delicious soup from stones, this strategy enables students to understand that each of us has a role in mentoring the other and contributing to the learning of the classroom. In the folktale, strangers arrive in a village carrying a pot containing only stones and water. The strangers tell the villagers that the stones will make a delicious soup. As the water boils around the stones, the strangers convince the villagers to each contribute something to the pot…just to make the soup a little better. Of course, once the villagers have all contributed a potato, a turnip, a cabbage, an onion, a carrot, and more, the soup becomes richer and the final result is a delicious vegetable broth.

In the classroom, students are asked to bring something to contribute to the Stone Soup. There is always a variety of vegetables that arrive and all are added to the pot. A few extra carrots or onions ensure that those who are not able to contribute, or who have forgotten to bring something, are able to share in the activity. The pot is set to boil on the staffroom stove, overseen by parent volunteers armed with some salt and pepper.

THROUGH THE WINDOW…

The desks in the classroom have been moved to form a long diagonal line from one corner of the classroom to the other so that all students can sit *at the same table* to share a meal.

The story has been read aloud and the students eagerly await the soup. In a classroom of twenty-five students, the servings are small, but when they are accompanied by some bread or crackers and students' personal lunches, the students enjoy their Stone Soup. It becomes a symbol of how, as a collaborative classroom of students and teacher who consistently communicate openly and mentor each other, much can be achieved. The richness of the broth changes from year to year, but there is never any soup left in the bowls. This is *their* soup! The spirit of collaboration and the contributions of each student ensure the celebration of a community effort. Each brings their gifts for the benefit of all.

ACTION STRATEGY: STONE SOUP

What…

Stone Soup is a traditional European folktale that describes how a group of hungry strangers claim they can make soup from stones when villagers refuse to feed them. As the water boils around the stones, the strangers invite villagers to add to the soup. As villagers bring in assortment of vegetables, of course, the broth becomes quite tasty. The story of stone soup represents the value of working together and supporting each other. Students see that what they contribute to the classroom becomes learning for all.

Implementation

How…

The process begins with a read-aloud of the story "Stone Soup". Being a traditional European folktale, there are various versions available in local libraries or online. After reading the story, the teacher suggests that the class make stone soup. Students are invited to bring a vegetable (each brings what they can) to contribute to the soup. In a class of 25 students, the selection of vegetables will ensure that a pot of soup will be tasty. It is best with a vegetable or chicken broth. Adding lots of onions, carrots, celery, garlic, herbs (basil, oregano, and parsley) and spices (cumin, paprika, salt, and pepper) will make a great soup. Other vegetables such as potatoes, corn, green beans, and diced tomatoes will add to the flavor. (Beware of student allergies, particularly in the use of spices and herbs.) Parent volunteers will be required to oversee the preparation of the soup on the staffroom stove or in crock pots. The portions can be small, but enough for every student to enjoy a taste. Starting with approximately 2 liters of liquid (just over 2 quarts) will yield 12 cups of soup as the cooking vegetables add liquid to the pot. You can increase or decrease depending on how much soup you plan to serve each student. Generally ½ cup of soup as an accompaniment to students' regular lunch makes a great tasting adventure. As the students enjoy their soup, the teacher encourages students to see the analogy between contributing to the soup and contributing to the classroom learning. When each participant brings what they can, the soup/learning is much better.

Why…

Students mentoring each other transforms a classroom of 1 teacher and 25 students into a classroom of 26 ongoing learners who support each other and collaboratively enhance the learning for all. Stone Soup heightens confidence that students gain as learners when they realize they are also supporting or mentoring the learning of others, allowing the success of each student to contribute to the success of all.

What If…

What if the consistent message in every lesson was the value of students mentoring each other, collaborating in learning, sharing their understandings, and working together to enrich learning for the whole classroom community?

There is nothing more gratifying for a teacher than to meet up with a student years later and hear about how they were inspired by the learning that was shared in the classroom. Yet even if our paths never cross again, we can all be that teacher for the students in our classrooms. We know the qualities that make a great teacher — the teacher who cares, who builds relationships, and who supports learners. Each of us can be that teacher!

Your legacy is what you bring to the young minds that you inspire to wonder, create, problem-solve, and reach beyond by considering "what if" thinking, challenging current ways of doing, and opening new pathways to being in the world. You may never hear about it; you may never be invited to surprise a former student on *Oprah* when they make their mark on the world. However, never doubt that you have the potential to make a difference in what a child brings to the future. It is a huge responsibility, a great privilege, and a blessing bestowed on all teachers.

Conclusion

This book began with the story of my experience in a grade 2 classroom on September 11th, 2001, a tragic day in modern history. The experience led me to ask questions about teaching, about learning, about relationship and community, and about communication and collaboration.

More than twenty years later, I have much more experience in education, some of which I have shared in these pages, but I still have questions. I hope that I always will. It is the questions that motivate me to keep learning, to explore further, and to create new understandings.

I don't always find answers to the questions I have. The exploration of the questions and the insights that result, the understandings that develop, and the new questions that emerge, inspire me to keep seeking, learning, and, indeed, questioning. It is a never-ending cycle of learning.

In this book I hope that you have found some new ideas and strategies. I hope that you question them as you read and in doing so transform them into something that works for you as a teacher within the unique dynamic that marks every group of students in every classroom.

There is nothing more satisfying for me than watching students engage with the learning and make it their own. I love to see them take responsibility for thinking more deeply and exploring new areas of interest. No teacher can possibly ever teach a student all they need to know, but if we motivate them to love learning, communicate and share their understandings, and work collaboratively in community with others, they will have all they need to become tomorrow's leaders, thinkers, and concerned citizens.

What a unique gift for teachers…to make a difference in the lives of their students…and through them the world!

I wish you much joy in your teaching, peace in your classroom, and many, many questions.

References

Britton, J. (1970/1993). *Language and learning: The importance of speech in children's development* (2nd ed.). Portsmouth, NH: Boynton/Cook Publishers.

Brown, M. W. (1949). *The important book.* New York: Harper Collins.

Bruner, J. S. (1966). *Toward a theory of instruction.* Cambridge, MA: Harvard University Press.

Cazden, C. B. (1988). *Classroom discourse: The language of teaching and learning.* Portsmouth, NH: Heinemann.

Center on the Developing Child, Harvard University (2023). *Key concepts – resilience.* https://developingchild.harvard.edu/science/key-concepts/resilience/)

Dewey, J. (1916/1997). *Democracy and education: An introduction to the philosophy of education.* New York: Free Press.

Einstein, A., and Russell, B. (1955). *Russell-Einstein manifesto.* London.

Gee, J.P. (2008). *Social linguistics and literacies: Ideology in discourses* (3rd ed.). New York: Routledge.

Gibbs, J. (1987). *Tribes: A new way of learning and being together.* Santa Rosa, CA: CenterSource Systems LLC.

Government of Canada (2021). Truth and Reconciliation Commission Calls to Action. Education for Reconciliation. https://www.rcaanc-cirnac.gc.ca/eng/1524504501233/1557513602139

Institute for Integrative Science and Health (n.d). "Two-Eyed Seeing". Retrieved January 2023. http://www.integrativescience.ca/Principles/TwoEyedSeeing/

Lee, H. (1960). *To kill a mockingbird.* Philadelphia, PA: J.P. Lippincott and Co.

Livni, E. (2016). "The Japanese practice of 'forest bathing' is scientifically proven to improve your health". https://qz.com/804022/health-benefits-japanese-forest-bathing

Lorbiecki, M. (1998). *Sister Anne's hands.* New York: Puffin Books.

McAuliffe, C. (1985). Interview on *Today.* https://news.yahoo.com/1985-christa-mcauliffe-tells-today-120715960.html

Merriam-Webster Dictionary (2023). "Stewardship". https://www.merriam-webster.com/dictionary/stewardship

Michaels, S., O'Connor, C., and Resnick, L. (2008). "Reasoned participation: Accountable talk in the classroom and in civic life". *Studies in Philosophy and Education*, 27 (4), 283-297.

Moss, J. (1989). *One small voice.* Brooklyn, NY: Festival Attractions Inc.

Nickel, R. (2022). "Cold and hungry: Food inflation bites Canada's north". https://www.reuters.com/world/americas/cold-hungry-food-inflation-bites-canadas-north-2022-08-08/

Numeroff, L. (1991). *If you give a moose a muffin.* New York: Harper Collins.

Ontario Ministry of Education (2006). *The Ontario curriculum, grades 1-8, language* (Revised). Toronto: Author.

Ontario Ministry of Education (2016). *The kindergarten program.* Toronto: Author.

Palmer, P. J. (1998). *The courage to teach: Exploring the inner landscape of a teacher's life.* San Francisco: Jossey-Bass.

Parker, L., and Vetter, D. (2020). *Mentoring each other: teachers listening, learning and sharing to create more successful classrooms.* Markham, ON: Pembroke Publishers.

Paulsen, G. (2008). *Hatchet.* New York: Simon & Schuster.

Pearson, E. (2002). *Ordinary Mary's extraordinary deed.* Layton, Utah: Gibbs Smith.

Piaget, J. (1923/1959). *The language and thought of the child* (M. Gabain, R Gabain, trans.). New York: Routledge. (Original work published 1923.)

Quebec Education (2022). *Literacy today: A community of talk.* https://www. literacytoday.ca/home/blogs-and-newsletters/talk/a-community-of-talk

Schimmel, S. (1994). *Dear children of the earth.* Minnetonka, MN: NorthWord Press.

Schwartz, S., and Bone, M. (1995). *Retelling, relating, reflecting: Beyond the 3 R's.* Toronto: Nelson Thomson Learning Publishing.

Shakespeare, W. (1597). *Romeo and Juliet.*

Shankar, S. (2022) *What is self-regulation?* The Mehrit Center. https://self-reg.ca

Staniforth, S. (n.d.). *Get outdoors: An educator's guide to outdoor classrooms in parks, schoolgrounds and other special places.* http://www.metrovancouver. org/events/school-programs/K12publications/GetOutdoors.pdf

Stevens, C. (1971). *Peace train.* Santa Monica, CA: A&M Records.

Style, E. (1988). *Curriculum as window and mirror.* https://nationalseedproject. org/Key-SEED-Texts/curriculum-as-window-and-mirror

Taylor, C. (1992). *The house that crack built.* Vancouver, BC: Raincoast Books.

Van Camp, R. (2019). *May we have enough to share.* Victoria, B.C.: Orca Book Publishers.

Vasquez, V.M. (2003/2014). *Negotiating critical literacies with young children.* Mahwah, NJ: Lawrence Erlbaum Associates.

Vetter, D. (2008). "Towards a critical stance: Citizenship education in the classroom". In *Citizenship education in the era of globalization: Canadian Perspectives* (M. O'Sullivan and K. Pashby, eds., pp. 105-111). Rotterdam, Netherlands: Sense Publishing.

Vetter, D. (2009). *The impact of the implementation of Rich Talk Curriculum on the cross-curricular learning of grade 3 students* (PhD thesis). York University. https://library-archives.canada.ca/eng/services/services-libraries/theses/ Pages/item.aspx?idNumber=729988779

Vetter, D. (2014). "Bricks in a backpack: Respecting the invisible." *From the margins to the mainstream* (K. Cushner and J. Dowdy Lanham). ML: Rowan & Littlefield Education.

Vygotsky, L.S. (1986). *Thought and language* (A. Kozulin, trans.). Cambridge, MA: The MIT Press. (Original work published 1934.)

Wagamese, R. (2019). *One drum: Stories and ceremonies for a planet.* Vancouver, BC: Douglas & McIntyre.

White, E.B. (1952). *Charlotte's web.* New York: Harper and Brothers.

Wilder, L.I. (1992). *Little house on the prairie.* New York: Harper Collins.

Index

Action Strategies
  Anchor Books, 103
  Appreciations, 59–60
  Bringing It Back, 86–87
  Central Focus Design, 54–55
  Cross-Canada Tour, 93–94
  Curate and Critique, 20
  Glyphs, 41–42
  Happy Slippers Toolkit, 105–106
  Hear What I'm Thinking, 18
  Learning Paths, 36–37
  Lesson Baskets, 58
  Mathemagicians, 80–81
  Nature Nurtures, 112
  Noise Meter, 84
  Patterned Writing, 67–68
  Playing Card Groups, 56–57
  Podcasts, 48–49
  Publishing, 92–93
  Scaled Feedback, 35–36
  Stone Soup, 116
  Talk Shows, 34
  Talking to Learn, 16–17
  Thinking Journeys, 113–114
  Treasure Map to Learning, 22–23
  Turning to Wonder, 45
  Ways of Knowing, 78–79
  Welcoming Voices, 24–25
  What I Bring, 26–28
  What I Know, 65–66
  Wonder Walls, 110
Anchor Books
  action strategy, 103
  described, 102–104
Appreciations, 59–60
assessment, 12, 69–72
audit trails, 113
authentic, relevant, meaningful, purposeful talk
  authentic, 35
  described, 33
  explorations, 39
  knowings, 37–38
  Learning Paths, 36–39
  meaningful, 35
  new wonderings, 39
  purposeful, 35
  Q Chart, 38
  relevant, 35
  rich talk, 33
  role-play, 33–34
  scaled feedback, 35–36
  sharing, 39
  Talk Shows, 34
  wonderings, 38

Bricks in a Backpack, 44
Bringing It Back, 86–87

Calls to Action, 108
Central Focus Design
  action strategy, 54–55
  described, 53–54
central focus table, 59
citizenship
  Calls to Action, 108
  described, 100, 107
  innovative thinking, 109–110
  numerals, 107
  roles and responsibilities, 107
  social justice issues, 108–109
  Wonder Walls, 110
classroom resources, 19, 56, 57, 60–61, 91–92
collaboration
  confidence, 21–22
  context, 21–22
  critical thinking, 19
  Curate and Critique, 19–21
  equity and inclusion, 40–46
  independent thinking, 21
  isolation, 19
  questioning, 12–13
  technology, 67–69
  Treasure Map to Learning, 22–23
  value of, 19–20
co-mentoring, 74

communication
    changes in, 13
    cognitive development, 17
    Hear What I'm Thinking, 18
    importance of, 14
    learning to talk, 14, 15
    questioning, 12–13
    talking to learn, 14–17
community
    conflict resolution, 29
    controlling voices, 25
    facilitating success, 23–24
    flexible relationships, 26
    identifying strengths, 26
    independence, 28
    obstacles, 24
    providing opportunities, 29–30
    questioning, 12–13
    student responsibility, 28
    teacher intervention, 26
    Welcoming Voices, 24–25
    What I Bring, 26–28
comprehension levels, 72
confidence, 21–22, 26, 85, 102
conflict resolution, 29
context, 21–22
critical thinking, 19, 33, 38, 71, 72, 109
Cross-Canada Tour, 93–94
cross-curricular links, 93–94
Curate and Critique
    action strategy, 20
    described, 19–21
curriculum, 88–91

differentiated instruction, 87, 88, 95
digital resources, 62–63
Discourse, 14

educative talk, 14
empathy, 44, 102, 106, 108
engaged learning community
    Bringing It Back, 86–87
    classroom management, 81–82
    Cross-Canada Tour, 93–94
    cross-curricular links, 93–94
    engaging students' interests and ideas, 90–91
    living curriculum, 88–90
    Noise Meter, 84
    opening possibilities for classroom resources, 91–92
    publishing, 92–93
    relationship, 82–83

    responsibility, 83–85
    routines, 85–88
    teacher leadership, 94–95
engaging students' interests and ideas, 90–91
equitable learning, 64–66
equity and inclusion in collaborative learning
    bricks in a backpack activity, 44
    equal access, 43
    glyphs, 41–42
    icebreaker activities, 40–41
    inclusive activities, 42–44
    students' names, 40
    teacher as model, 40
    turning to wonder, 44–46
explorations, 35, 39

Glyphs
    action strategy, 41–42
    described, 41

Happy Slippers Toolkit, 105–106
Hear What I'm Thinking, 18

imaginary activities, 43
independence, 21, 28, 60, 83
isolation, 19

knowings, 36, 37–38
knowledge, 37

Learning Paths
    action strategy, 36–37
    described, 36, 37–39
learning to talk, 14, 15
legacy, 100, 111–117
Lesson Baskets, 58

Mathemagicians, 80–81
mentor teachers, 46
mentoring partnerships
    classroom communities, 46
    classroom stories, 47
    described, 46
    facilitating peer mentoring, 47
    mentor teachers, 46
    podcasts, 48–49
    social issues, 48
    students as mentors, 49
mentors, 23, 26, 49

Nature Nurtures, 112

new wonderings, 37, 39
Noise Meter, 84

online instructional space, 63–64

Patterned Writing, 67–68
peer feedback, 35–36
physical activity, 107
physical classroom environment
    Appreciations, 59–60
    book crates, 55–56
    bulletin boards, 60–61
    central focus design, 53–55
    central focus table, 59
    circle conversations, 60
    friends, 56
    Lesson Baskets, 57–58
        objective, 53
        Playing Card Groups, 56–57
        seating plan, 56
        storage, 55–56
        student-centred approach, 53–54
        students' interests and experiences, 61
        working group, 56
    Playing Card Groups
        action strategy, 56–57
        described, 56, 57
    Podcasts
        action strategy, 48–49
        described, 48
    publishing, 92–93

Q Chart, 38
questioning
    assessment, 12
    collaboration, 19–23
    communication, 14–18
    community, 23–29
    described, 11–13
    research, 13–14

relationship, 82–83
research, 13–14
resilience, 101
responsibility, 83–85
rich talk, 33
role-play, 33–34
routines, 85–88

Scaled Feedback, 35–36
self-efficacy, 102

self-regulation, 104–106
sharing, 37, 39
Show and Tell, 11
social interaction, 19
social justice issues, 108–109
speech, 18
stewardship
    audit trails, 113
    collaboration, 111
    described, 100, 111, 113
    outdoor time, 111–112
    space program, 113
    Stone Soup, 115–116
    teachers' roles, 114–117
    Thinking Journeys, 113–114
Stone Soup
    action strategy, 116
    described, 115
student engagement, 88, 90–91
student responsibility, 28
students' interests and ideas, 90–91

Talk Shows, 34
Talking to Learn
    action strategy, 16–17
    described, 14, 15
    gap between theory and implementation, 15–16
teacher leadership, 94–95
technology and community
    assessment, 69–72
    availability, 62
    collaboration, 67–69
    described, 61
    digital resources, 62–63
    equitable learning, 64–66
    funding, 62
    online instructional space, 63–64
    Patterned Writing, 67–68
    What I Know, 65–66
thinking about thinking
    alternative ways of knowing, 78
    individual learning, 77–78
    Mathemagicians, 80–81
    memorization, 75
    past experiences, 80
    peer thinking, 77
    perspective, 79–80
    remembering, 75
    resource availability, 80
    source acknowledgement, 79
    subtraction, 77

thinking, 75–76
    Ways of Knowing, 78–79
Thinking Journeys, 113–114
Treasure Map to Learning, 22–23
Turning to Wonder
    action strategy, 45
    described, 44, 45–46

voice, 90

Ways of Knowing, 78–79
Welcoming Voices, 24–25
well-being
    Anchor Books, 102–104
    described, 100–101

empathy, 102, 106
Happy Slippers Toolkit, 105–106
physical activity, 107
relationship building, 101
reminders of success, 106–107
resilience, 101
self-efficacy, 102
self-regulation, 104–106
stress control strategies, 106
What I Bring, 26–28
What I Know, 65–66
Wonder Walls, 110
wonderings, 36, 37
worry stones, 105–106